Trudi Sorensen

Trudi Sorensen
5/26/77

CREATIVE MOTION

CREATIVE MOTION

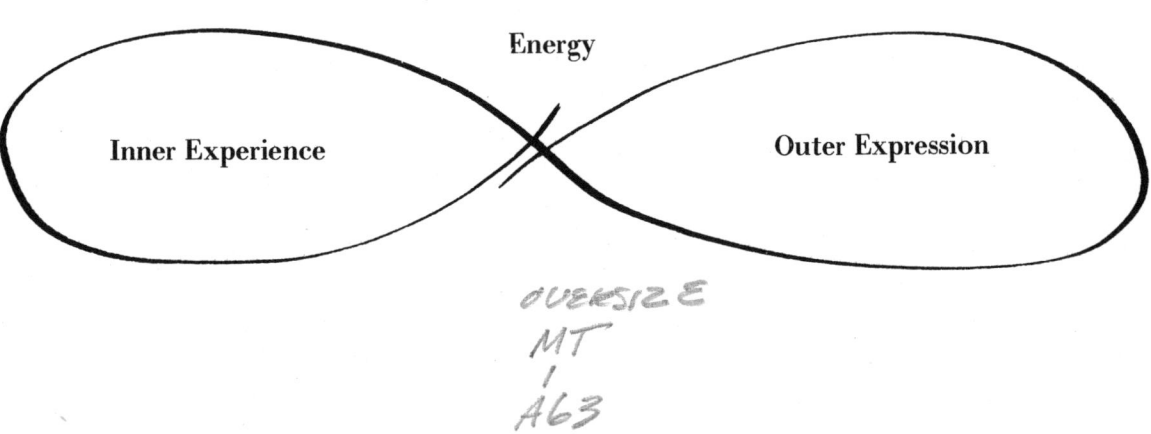

Published By
DROKE HOUSE, PUBLISHERS
Anderson, S. C.
✱✱✱

CREATIVE MOTION
Copyright, © 1971 by Margaret Allen and Anne Niles

All Rights Reserved

No part of this book may be reproduced or transmitted in any form or by any means, electronic or mechanical, including photocopying, or by any information storage or retrieval system, without permission in writing from the publisher.

First Edition

Standard Book Number: 8375-6753-X

Library of Congress Catalog Card Number: 78-121094

Manufactured In The United States of America

Published by
DROKE HOUSE, Publishers
116 West Orr Street
Anderson, S.C. 29621

To the memory of

OPAL

Our thanks for making this publication possible

to

Ann Haworth   Meredith Gilpatrick

and all those whose faith in Creative Motion
has given us the courage to write this book.

Margaret Allen
Anne Niles

ACKNOWLEDGMENTS

We have had the good fortune to review the scientific aspects of Creative Motion with Thomas Strickler, chairman of the department of Physics at Berea College, Berea, Kentucky. Our hours of conversation with Dr. Strickler helped to illucidate these concepts as they relate to Motion.

Without the dedicated help of Phylis (Mrs. Richard) Hinchman of Groton, Massachusettes, who typed Margaret Allen's share of the manuscript, this part of the project would not have been so happily and efficiently accomplished.

Professor Helen May of Johnson College, Johnson, Vermont and Professor Robert Lewis of Berea College, who, with a sensitive eye, read the manuscript with particular attention to its clarity.

For the illustrations we are greatly indebted to Billy Davis, director of photography of the Louisville Courier Journal, to Warren Brunner of the Brunner Studio in Berea, and to John Roberts of New Albany, Indiana.

Margaret Allen
Anne Niles

PREFACE

Young babies, learning to stand and walk, often respond to music by springing up and down, doing a baby dance of whole motion. In primitive tribes, too, music is unseparated from dance. There is a wholeness of response that is lost in most of us. With us, education and custom bring about an unequal division of our faculties. We lay great stress upon intellectual gains. We get much of our instruction about music sitting in orderly rows of desks in classrooms, and we are seldom expected to transfer anything we learn into physical action. We come to speak of music in abstract ways with numbers and letters — the fourth measure, the second phrase, the B section — forgetting that unless music says something closer to our feelings, it could not endure.

It must be granted that, in many ways, making music must be an athletic activity. A pianist needs power, speed, accuracy, endurance, efficiency of motion — all athletic skills. Yet we do not train our musicians bodies as athletes do. Our training is fragmented. We concentrate on the fingers, the hand, at most the arm or torso; we do not work with the whole self.

When someone, especially a young inexperienced student, makes music that is exciting and alive, we call him, without knowing what we mean exactly, a talented student. Talent has never been adequately defined. It remains a vague concept that needs to be retired from use. It may well be, however, that the student whom we call talented is one who has not fragmented his abilities, one who responds whole — with body, mind and feeling. He may be one who has not learned the unnatural distinction of categories like physical, mental and emotional.

If so, talent is available to us all. With Creative Motion principles, we have the techniques to regain the lost wholeness of response that we had as babies. And as music teachers, we need not merely enjoy our talented students and tolerate our untalented ones. Each student becomes a hopeful challenge, since we have in our hands a way of teaching the expression of music as an experience based on the fundamental princples of our use of energy.

Don Pease
Atlanta,
August, 1970

CONTENTS

INTRODUCTION ... 13

PART ONE

THE SOURCE *Anne Niles*
- Martha Russell's Search ... 15
- Horace Mann Experiment ... 17
- Teaching and Students ... 18
- Windswept Music Workshop ... 20

CREATIVE MOTION *Anne Niles* ... 23
- Origin of Name ... 24
- The Development ... 24
- Energy Use – Timing ... 25
- Harnessing the Yawn ... 26
- Light Weight Body ... 28
- Experience and Expression

PART TWO

APPLYING CREATIVE MOTION TO THE TEACHING OF MUSIC *Margaret Allen* ... 45
- Creative Motion Learning ... 46
- The Instrument ... 49
- The Ear Approach ... 51
- The Eye Approach ... 55
- Note Value Timing ... 59
- Intervals ... 67
- Harmonic Beats ... 71
- The Metric Wave ... 87
- Phrase Form ... 90
- Ourselves in Relation to Phrase ... 96
- Suggestions to Teachers ... 97
- Suggestions on Analysis ... 99

PART THREE

FURTHER THOUGHTS
- Adult Class Remarks *Opal Gilpatrick* ... 131
- Snowball Exercise *Opal Gilpatrick* ... 133
- How Parents Can Help the Learning Process *Florice Tanner* ... 133
- Applying Creative Motion In The Classroom *Florice Tanner* and *Julia Ostergaard* ... 135
- Reading Aloud *Julia Ostergaard* ... 136
- New Responsibilities *Florice Tanner* and *Julia Ostergaard* ... 136

Body Tuning *Martha Russell*

SUPPLEMENT
    Chart — Breaks and Arches   139
    General Exercises Used in Creative Motion Work   140
    Flat-Finger Work *Martha Russell*   141
    Light Weight Body Maintenance *Martha Russell*   148
    Thiensville Experimental School Report   150
    Horace Mann Study Report   150
    Baltimore Group Report   152

About The Authors

Introduction

Many musicians in recent years have sought to vitalize traditional playing of music. Among such exponents was Martha Stockton Russell of Evanston, Illinois, who early in the twenties initiated a basic change in approach, the principles of which she termed *Creative Motion*. In the three decades that followed, Mrs. Russell gathered around her many dedicated students, those who felt the impact of her genius and strove to carry out her principles at whatever level they might have been teaching. Today, some of those original students are joining together to offer the present volume. Though this work is composed of the writings of several persons, the outlook and method of the authors represent a single enterprise with a single goal to expound the unique principles of Creative Motion.

The principles of Creative Motion, being ahead of their time and subsequently established, still are not accepted by the musico-academic world today. For a generation Mrs. Russell and her students have demonstrated the superior character of inner-directed musicianship in both private and public training, as well as in special courses in a variety of schools (see details in Supplement section). Each of the respective accounts has been derived from the letters, notes and teaching of Martha Russell and Opal Gilpatrick, with personal adaptation developed through individual experience and inspired by participation in many Windswept Music Workshops.

In the dispersive and chaotic age which we are living through, much criticism is being directed at the permissive upbringing of the children of the post-World War II years. Consequently, today there is a pressing need for self-directed action and expression, which the principles of Creative Motion have proved to effect.

Part One, *The Source and Creative Motion,* was written by Anne Niles, with the encouragement and help of Rachel Sherman of Columbus, Ohio. Anne began her studies with Mrs. Russell in 1920 while a senior in the Bryn Mawr School. With growing enthusiasm she followed the development of the work and later assisted in Mrs. Russell's Baltimore classes. Since that time she has continued to teach the body tuning work and to take an active part in the Windswept Workshops.

Part Two, *Creative Motion in the Teaching of Music,* was written by Margaret Allen, who was both traditionally and creatively trained in music. Possessing an innate ability to improvise, from the age of ten she was teaching harmony to her playmates. Her undergraduate training in music consisted of three years at Oberlin College, with graduation from the University of Wisconsin. Her study of Creative Motion began with two winters study with Martha Russell and a summer school session at La Jolla, California. Then in her large classes in Westchester, New York, she used Creative Motion as the fundamental approach. Later she received from Stanford University her Masters degree in Education, and for twenty-five years has been Professor of Humanities and Piano at Berea College, Kentucky. For nineteen years she has been the moving force that has made possible the Windswept Music Workshop, where each summer an increasing number of students and teachers from many sections of the country have gathered to take part in the significant program of Creative Motion training.

Part Three, *Further Thoughts*, consists of Opal Gilpatrick's notes, teaching suggestions and exercises; then follow the application of Creative Motion principles to help parents and teachers by Florice Tanner of Waynesville, North Carolina and Julia Ostergaard of Evanston, Illinois, both formerly teachers in Winnetka, Illinois elementary schools; it ends with a summary of the training and its purpose by Martha Russell.

In the *Supplement* may be found General Physical Exercises and Flat Finger Piano Exercises by Mrs. Russell, followed by a resume of some private school Creative Motion classes.

The book was undertaken as an answer to a mounting demand by those studying and teaching Creative Motion, who desired a source book. It is essentially a series of variations upon the central theme of the principles involved. Finally, these principles offer the reader an opportunity to grow in awareness of the fundamental interplay of mental and physical energy necessary for enhanced performance and satisfaction in every form of activity.

PART ONE

THE SOURCE
Anne Niles

When Martha Stockton was born in 1875, her father was a veteran of the Union Army, with bitter memories, and a bad wound that gave him trouble for the rest of his life. His greatest pleasure was singing, with accompaniment on his guitar, to his appreciative, brown-eyed, little daughter. Later he showed her simple chord patterns so that she could play the songs for herself on the piano. This was the beginning of joy.

Most of the father's favorite songs were Irish or Scottish with a wonderful lilt and swing. They were later written down and harmonized by the daughter and recorded, along with folksongs from many lands, in her book *Sing Swing and Play*.[1]

In the preface to that small volume, Martha Stockton Russell tells the story of what happened to that happy little girl when she was allowed to begin to study music.

"It was not until she was seven that she had her first piano lesson. She had looked forward so long to that day that when at last it came she climbed the teacher's steps with the feeling that the doors of paradise were swinging wide. And then, instead of the singing, moving beauty she had gone to find, she met little black notes (on the page) and shiny white keys (on the piano), and if you matched them fast enough, moved your fingers fleetly, and played with something that in those days was called 'expression' — that was music."

Martha never did learn to play very well herself, for a variety of reasons, but when she grew up she decided that "more than anything else, she wanted to know what it was that she had known as a little girl, and didn't know any more. What was the magic Something that sometimes got into music and made it come alive, but most of the time wasn't there at all? She had to know, and presently she started to find out."

This sensitive girl grew up in the sheltered, rather formal atmosphere of the '90s. Her wise mother, however, realizing that Martha needed to create beauty around her, allowed her to furnish and decorate her own little "House-Party" house, on her grandmother's place, in Sewickley, Pennsylvania, where they spent their summers. It was near Pittsburgh, on the Ohio River, where their ancestor,

1. Viking Press, 1938. Currently available from Anne Niles, 5600 Waycrest Lane, Baltimore, Md. 21210

General Leet, had been granted some acreage as a recompense for his service to the Continental Army by General Washington.

Martha lavished much care on the planning and preparation of delicacies for her guests. Everything had to be tasted and seasoned just right, for she was always a gourmet cook. Often there was dancing, when the young ladies with hair piled high were whirled around to the popular waltzes and polkas of the day, showing off their many ruffled petticoats. These were the carefree years.

All the while, Martha was spending a great deal of time reading. She loved fantasy in poetry and prose, but also read widely in history, biography and later in psychology and science. In this way, she early became aware of the problems outside her protected circle. She had tremendous empathy for people of every sort. In fact, friends often hesitated to tell her of any suffering, because she so evidently identified with every painful detail.

Martha was never robust herself, but her enthusiasm for life enabled her to rise above physical limitations. After a wonderfully happy marriage to Frank Russell and the birth of two boys, it became necessary for her to undergo thyroid surgery. Indeed, it was while she was in the hospital, struggling to recover, that the awful news of her husband's sudden death was brought to her.

Even before that tragedy, she and her young husband had watched, helplessly, as their older boy literally faded away, at the age of two and a half. In those days insulin had not yet been discovered to control diabetes. Now only frail little Christopher was left to her for a few brief years.

From this little one she learned that music directly affects the body reactions of the young child. By his happy crowing or symptoms of distress, Christopher showed, even as an infant, what sort of music his mother was playing. This knowledge sent her forth to search out ways of re-opening contact with music in older children who had lost their original ability to respond directly, inhibited perhaps by competition with playmates and the demands of an adult world. With characteristic determination she set out to find answers to this problem.

She had already graduated from Northwestern University's Music Theory Department, but now she went to London to study with Dr. Yorke at the Royal Academy of Music. Still not satisfied, she went to work with Jacques Dalcroze in Hellerau, Germany. This time she acquired a new awareness of the importance of the body, as well as the mind and spirit, in any form of creative expression.

Gradually her own techniques evolved. She began by teaching group singing, and a modified Dalcroze method, in a number of schools. Each school was chosen for purposes of observation, experiment and demonstration connected with her research. She taught at the Latin School in Chicago, 1914-1916; the Park School, Buffalo, 1917-1918; and the Bryn Mawr School in Baltimore, 1919-1921.

Perhaps Bryn Mawr School's headmistress, Edith Hamilton, (better known in later years as the author of *The Greek Way* and other books,) was beginning to feel that her girls lacked something, when she asked her girlhood friend to introduce such a "frill" in her school. For it had been modelled upon the classical preparatory boys' schools of the period, and music must have been considered sissy.

Martha Russell presented music as an important fundamental for binding one's life into a unity. The relation of feeling to action, inside to outside, was something new to the usual concept of education. However, her teaching was apparently welcomed as a stabilizing force, and music has continued at the school ever since.

For the next ten years, La Jolla, California, was the locus of her work. There she gave private lessons, held a children's "Joy For A Penny" course and, especially important for the development of her teaching, a summer school workshop in Creative Motion, as she now called her method. To her lovely studio home near the sea, came students from many parts of the country to spend six weeks of intensive study in every aspect of music.

The necessity of involving the whole person, body, mind and spirit, in the production of music was perhaps her greatest contribution. One does not just put "expression" into his playing by dynamics or changes of tempo, he lives out the music with his entire body and the result is a true expression.

After a summer at the workshop, the students returned to teaching in places as far off as New England, Texas, Minnesota and Kentucky. Some of them taught music, others applied the principles of Creative Motion to the dramatic arts, to dancing, to physical education and even to the three R's.

The Depression forced the closing of this studio workshop series, but the work went on elsewhere. A private experimental school for the early grades was held at Thiensville, Wisconsin. Here even arithmetic was integrated with body work, through musical games, to give the child "concrete contact with numbers". They were taught "Don't throw the inner feeling of you-ness onto an external accomplishment. Stand free of the thing you do . . . Grade up to your own abilities and attainments. Each one of us goes on his own rhythm and on his own curve."[2]

Especially interesting was a controlled experiment in the second grade at the Horace Mann School in New York City. The children who were in a Creative Motion class for two half-hour periods a week, showed a marked improvement over the control group. To quote from the Conclusion of the Report of the Horace Mann Creative Motion Study.[3]

"The child has a strong desire for a definite, recognizable achievement of which he can be proud. It is tied up with his feeling of security, with his wanting to know 'where he is'. This is evidenced by his love of rules, patterns and repetitions. How to satisfy this need and yet not tangle him up in comparative evaluations of his results and abilities, comparisons which often lead to feelings of inadequacy and failure, is one of the big problems education faces."

" . . . In every instance it is evident that the growth of the child who had Motion work is pointed with awareness. He is cognizant of his own strength with which to meet these problems. He knows he is growing and in what direction. He is 'on top'."

Why Teachers College did not follow through with the implications of this study is not known. At the time the principal of Horace Mann, Rollo G. Reynolds wrote, "The increased well-being of the children to whom this special work was made available certainly holds significance for modern education!"

Like many people who had concern for the evolution of a decent society, Martha Russell, after the agony of World War II, was thrown back once again to question what was wrong with our civilization. Technology had certainly improved, but had man developed the resources to cope with his new problems?

For a long time now, she had observed that new babies were being born with a different head set and that this set probably presaged a new evolutionary step for man's body. Comparing pictures of infants and young children in the 20's and 30's with Victorian baby pictures, she found a higher, more

2. See Supplement p. 19 *Thiensville School* Report
3. Ibid. p. 18

erect carriage of the head, the occipital bones held higher above the spine.

Such a development necessitated a strong lower back in order to substantiate the new posture. Noting the universal slouch and frequent sacroilliac troubles so much in evidence, she could find no adjustment corresponding to the new evolutionary necessity. Tradition in the gymnasium and army posture still disregarded the problem, continuing to demand a raised chest with shoulders thrown back. Such posture was bound to cause back trouble in anyone as soon as he lost his prime muscle tone. That meant nearly everyone in our sedentary life and inadequate exercise.

She therefore developed some simple exercises,[4] beginning with correct breathing, to keep bodies aligned, free of tension and with proper utilization of energy. She used her knowledge of body balances, opposition of forces and rhythmic flow, not merely for musical proficiency, but to facilitate every form of activity.

It was deplorable she felt, that the child of school age should lose the ease and wholeness of functioning that he had had from birth. Wherever she went, she tried to make teachers responsive to the danger especially in the early grades in school, while the children's bodies are still pliable.

In the preface to *Sing, Swing, Play,* Mrs. Russell describes her original music finding,

" . . . an inner beat in the music that hides itself in the count of the measure rhythm and matches a tiny pulse vibration at the center of the diaphragm, that big springboard in the body where the crura muscles cross. This pulse vibration is touched off by the inner beat in the music, and that "Something" which is released tunes our body instrument to vibrate exactly with the beat of the music we play or sing."

"Harmonic Beat" she came to call this fundamental pulse, for it occurs at the place in the music where the harmony "swings". It is the heart-beat, as it were, that gives life to the music. These beats pile up into phrase, as one feels the ebb and flow of the composition, so that the music breathes, coming alive for both performer and listener.

In teaching, her emphasis was on "inside singing". One must hear-feel the music and match the music's requirements. The whole body of the player must be synchronized with the music, before he is allowed to touch the keys. Practice time was greatly shortened but was intensive. Each lesson brought deeper realization of the piece.

No matter how far away her students were, Martha Russell kept in touch with those who were doing the Motion work. She travelled widely to spend a few days coaching and sharing her discoveries. These visits were highly prized. When personal lessons were not possible, letters would have to suffice; explaining difficulties and offering new insights. Even after she settled in Baltimore, because of her need to be near the Johns Hopkins Hospital for medical consultation and tests, she continued active teaching.

There was a large class of adults as well as an experimental group of 10 boys and girls. These children, recruited from five local private schools, came for an hour once a week. There was a psychological evaluation at the start and at the end of the school year. The final report showed improvement in personality and feelings of belonging in all the children. To quote from the psychologist's letter: "I was particularly impressed by the fact that, in general, all the changes indicated were in the direction of more acceptable behavior and more wholesome attitudes both towards self and towards social situations."[5] This was an interesting result to come from what to the

4. Physical Exercises, Supplement, p. 1
5. Baltimore Group Letter. Supplement p. 20

children seemed to be body tuning and fun with music.

At this time she also worked to complete her book, *A Music Lens On History*[6] despite time out for cataract operations. She was never satisfied with the manuscript, but the book was printed after her death through the interest of friends to whom she had read many of the chapters.

Teaching remained her forte, whether to individuals or groups. She never seemed to be tired after a long lesson, rather she apparently derived strength from teaching. In fact she was on a round of visits to the Chicago area in 1951, teaching still, when the end came.

The work went on in a number of places. In Winnetka, Illinois, there were two alert friends who had profitted from Martha Russell's experience and observations. One was Florice Tanner who went from class to class working with different groups of children, increasing their awareness of how they organized themselves for various kinds of school activities. She also taught them proper body balances at easle and work bench in arts and crafts and shop work. Since she had a relatively free relationship with the children, she found many opportunities to develop ways of achieving proper readiness and control of energy, so that they directed their own activities and made their own plans to a great extent. Creative Motion principles were important in what she accomplished.

Cooperating with Florice, was Julia Ostergaard, an experienced first grade teacher, who applied the same principles to her classroom teaching. The quiet poise and strength these children showed during their first year of real schoolwork, was extraordinary. They were very eager, yet able to *use* their eagerness to effect the results they wished to achieve.

These two teachers collaborated in writing up their experiments and results in several papers.[7] Although they were successful in freeing children's bodies, giving them good control and at the same time reducing disciplinary problems, their methods were never adopted by other teachers or encouraged by the management. It is hard to introduce something new into any system!

Among Martha Russell's loyal followers, Opal Gilpatrick was the most dedicated teacher. She heard about the La Jolla summer school from her conservatory teacher. Because she was still in quest of something deeper than anything she had yet experienced, she took the long trip to California. There she found Creative Motion, which immediately became her life's work.

Wherever she lived, eager pupils flocked to her because of the unique quality of her teaching. Their parents, too, were stimulated by the depth of her approach and her contribution to the musical life of the community.

She was equally successful with every age, from toddlers, who had to sit on several fat volumes to reach the keys, through school and conservatory bound young people. Teachers came to her as well to learn her way and follow to the Summer Workshops. Each student, according to his talent, developed remarkable ease at the piano and great sensitivity of tone.

In addition to these lessons in her home studio, Opal carried the motion work to many pre-school classes in Columbus, Ohio. Although she often found tense little bodies and balky behavior at first, she soon got them to loosen up and respond freely and joyously to the music, literally flowing around the room, like a flock of birds.

There was never a more radiant teacher; sympathetic, enthusiastic, everlastingly patient. She kept on working until the student got the experience. He had to play to the "best of his ability at the

6. A Music Lens On History by Martha S. Russell. Lucas Bros. Baltimore 1952
7. See Further Thoughts

moment". Trying was not enough.

In every way Opal contributed to the understanding of Creative Motion. She made talks to parents and other groups; conducted workshops for teachers and kept note books, hoping until her death in 1968 to write. Without her inspiration and patient work this volume could never have been undertaken.

It would be impossible to write about the Source of Creative Motion without also describing the Windswept Music Workshop, located twelve miles from Berea, Kentucky, where the work is being carried on every June in a unique way. This workshop has continued for nineteen years because of the phenomenal energy, imagination and skill of Margaret Allen. Her mountaintop acres have been well named *Keys of Heaven* by her Appalachian neighbors, for the wide sweep of sky, the meadowed valley and the waves of hills lead the eye into far horizons. Sometimes mysterious mountain peaks appear to float like islands, in the morning mist. Amid this beauty Mrs. Allen has built cabins to house the growing needs of the Workshop and shared with Opal Gilpatrick the teaching responsibilities. From fifty to sixty teachers and students are accomodated for a week of music study according to the principles of Creative Motion as developed by Martha Russell.

These principles define the feeling structure of music and describe the process through which this structure can be expressed. It is a process with the emphasis upon the realization of the music idea: technique and interpretation evolving as a single whole, rather than the training with which we are all familiar; that of learning a technique and then interpreting the music afterwards. Creative Motion is a new dimension in learning. This teaching and playing is inclusive of a deep understanding of the musical intent and content of the composer, so that each performance is a re-creative experience, not a repetition.

At Windswept, from the singing of Bach chorales before breakfast, to the parting hymn in the evening, the focus is on experience. Daily classes include body tuning, which is putting all the elements of music (note value, rhythm, interval, phrase) into action or body response; a coaching or class criticism period for piano students; a seminar for advanced students and teachers, in the techniques of teaching. The evenings are filled with group singing, under a choral director, or listening to the performance of advanced students. Along with all these activities, the younger students spend their afternoons preparing an operetta, which will be performed on the last evening. It is done in pantomime, using the body responses demanded by the timing of the music. The scenery and props are miracuously executed on the premises, adding a whimsical touch of make believe against the natural beauty of the surroundings.

Attending the Workshop is a rewarding experience in many ways: the mountain-top serenity, the expressed beauty of the ordinary details of living and the impact of the group's sharing vital learning makes it so.

The following are quotations from letters written to Margaret Allen by some of the students, after a Workshop exerpience.

"I am really looking forward to this year's Windswept. I don't think I could help coming. The atmosphere there is one which can't be found any other place in the world!"

"I enjoyed Windswept more than ever before. Next June will never come soon enough."

"You and the other teachers stimulated me to a level of courage which no one had ever done before. I was able to work hard at something without being forced into it. I put out energy for *Hansel and Gretel* and didn't know how easy it is to work. This feeling inside is the result of your work . . . the experience pointing out a whole new way of looking at things. Thank you for glowing!"

The lower terrace at dawn.

CREATIVE MOTION
Anne Niles

Everything we do, we do with our bodies! Does that seem like a startling statement? Then I would like you to try an experiment.

If I were to drop a book on the floor and then asked, "Without using your body, please pick up that book," you would probably reply, "That is impossible. I cannot do it."

Did you notice, however, that at my order your body *wanted* to do my command? The energy was mobilized and ready, but the execution was blocked by the limitation not to use your body. It was therefore a frustrating experience.

Much of the frustration you see in the bodies, the feet, the faces of the people you encounter shuffling along, or pounding the sidewalk as they go about the business of living, is related to a lack of knowledge of the fundamental use of energy in their bodies. "Do we move freely and joyfully within the universe, or do we resist that free flowing motion?" Opal Gilpatrick was fond of asking.

A number of teachers who have been exposed to the work developed by Martha Russell have been helping their students discover a more rewarding mode of living. They aim in their teaching to recover the apparently effortless motion possessed by animals, as well as little children, before they have begun to imitate their elders. Many of these people are music teachers, but others are working in kindergartens, elementary grades, or adult groups, or teaching activities of every sort. They use the principles discovered through music but applicable in any situation.

Motion and movement have generally been used as interchangeable terms, but, for our purpose, *movement* is change of place, the outside result of the use of energy; *motion*, on the other hand, has been called "an impulse to action; the inner working of a governing idea." (note) Defined thus, motion is the very essence of the process of proper functioning. It was therefore *Creative Motion* that Martha Russell called her way of teaching.

She used music in her teaching because music has to be created anew, through the body of the musician every time it is played. No intermediate material object or picture is interposed between performer and hearer. "Music itself," she said, "is just the sound of motion." Having her students match their body balances to the requirements of the demands of the music became the fundamental of her teaching.

She developed a special kind of in-depth Rhythm Class with precise body, leg, arm, and hand

Note: *Funk and Wagnall's Dictionary*, 1915.

balances corresponding to the different note values and rhythmic patterns. The harmonic color quality of tonic, dominant, major and minor chords was brought out in body equivalent. The dramatic expression values inherent in each composition were portrayed in motion; vital music using the big body muscles of legs and back; emotive, employing more subtle, inner shadings; the mental type of music being crisply articulated with the smaller muscles of hands and feet.

The inner pulse of the music was followed. She called the *Harmonic Beat,* the place where the music throbs, as it swings the cascade of melody. Then *Melodic Respiration,* the flow of the musical pitch on the pulse of the *Harmonic Beats,* was matched with *Lateral* or *Vertical* body balances. Tying everything together was the study of the phrasing, which gives form and meaning to a whole composition.

Before sitting down at the piano, the student analyses the music through experiencing the body balances that express the music. When the playing actually begins, diaphragm, head, legs, feet, as well as arms, hands, and fingers are coordinated by the inner hearing-feeling-singing of the now already somewhat familiar piece. The result is that there is a musical swing to the playing, even before the notes are thoroughly learned. Since the whole body is involved with respiring to the flow of the music, the motion of the music comes through and there is much less stumbling or groping for notes. The performer has the satisfaction of hearing himself *making music* to the best of his ability, at the moment.

Group singing is likewise based on extroversion through body balances. The phrasing is worked out to give inner meaning to the important words, without the use of mere *dynamic* accent. Studied in this way, a song gives tremendous musical satisfaction and growth, with a minimum of tiresome repetion.

After much reflection and study, Martha Russell concluded that it was the instinctive perfection of *timing* that marks the genius player. In essence timing, the synchronization of the working of the parts with the working of the whole, was his secret. We ordinarily reserve the concept of timing for use in athletics, but it is really the fundamental principle that relates our entire being to *any* activity. It is correct timing that makes the fine dancer, not counting 1-2-3 in a waltz, but moving to the wave of the music. Similarly, the good diver, the tennis player, the easy driver, the cook who can successfully produce an entire meal, even the mother who can call in the children without causing a disturbance in their rhythm of play, all these are using good timing in various ways. Even a machine cannot run properly without good timing. That is why we need to have our cars "tuned" as well as our pianos.

Hence, in working with Creative Motion it becomes obvious that timing is what really makes the difference between success and failure in all that we do. In our relations with each other, in diplomatic and business contacts, in teaching and in art we need good timing. But how do we learn it?

Returning, now, to the example used at the beginning of this chapter, let us see if you can have a concrete experience. You may actually use your body, this time, to pick up the book. Do it in slow motion, so that you can study the steps.

What happens when I say, "Pick up the book?" First you have the idea. You tell yourself, "I am going to pick up the book!" Then you observe that your body instantly gears for the act, i.e. *it is ready;* the necessary energy is mobilized.

Now be careful. If you hold onto that body gearing you will be tense about the task, and on the other hand, if you let out the "readiness" too soon, you will make hard going of the job. Here an important discovery can help.

At the impulse, or moment of initiating the action, you must "rest" that energy gearing at the diaphragm (the distribution center of your body) where a tiny down-up-and-away pulse vibration occurs. This gesture sends out the energy charge of your governing idea to the periphery of the body: the hands, feet, head, covering the specific act. At this point of impulse you carry out your idea, bending down to where the book lies on the floor.

As you grasp the book, you reach the climax of your act. Now release your breath, as well as the energy charge, and you will return without effort to a standing position, with the book in your hand.

The important steps are, first, knowing when you are ready, like saying "on your marks, get set" and the second is knowing how (it really amounts to being *willing*) to "rest" the "go" upon the cover of the flight to time the action. By taking that tiny pulse, like a bird's take-off, you achieve the relationship between yourself and your act. As Mr. Ossip Gabrilowitsch, the pianist-conductor, once said to Martha Russel, you will have "vitality coming from the point of relaxation!"

Finally, there is the release to the follow through, so often mentioned in golf lessons, but just as important in the smallest act of everyday. Without the release at the climax of your phrase, you will not be ready for the next thing to be done. You will, therefore, go around trailing unfinished business, which piles up tension and gives no satisfaction, even when many tasks have actually been accomplished.

One way to achieve phrasing, in sports or life is "Harnessing the Yawn". The yawn is the natural prototype of energy patterning in the body. It contains all the elements of phrasing: gearing-cover-impulse-release. Try opening the back of your throat, as if to say "Ah". Keep your lips closed, as you inhale. You will soon feel a yawn growing. Let it come, and when the actual yawn takes over, as it will, in a few seconds, notice what happens.

A mysterious energy charge goes instantly from the center of the body to the extremeties, filling the entire body the way a room fills with light the moment you press the light switch. The body then unfolds and stretches, filling out the extension to the maximum, until the climax of the yawn is reached. Sometimes tears fill the eyes, there is such a tremendous release throughout the body.

After a good yawn, one feels glowing all over. That feeling of "ah" should accompany every smallest act or gesture. By thus "harnessing" the yawn, one acquires inner equilibrium and a feeling of adequacy and relatedness. In Creative Motion classes, a yawn is encouraged as a sign that students are getting their bodies tuned and freed for action.

No doubt you are saying that it is considered rude to yawn — yes, that is true. Nonetheless the freeing of the diaphragm, through the use of the instinctive miracle of the yawn is the surest way to get ready for any task.

Ashley Montague, the anthropologist, points out that, contrary to popular belief, yawning is more of a waking-up process than a going-to-sleep one. He claims that any after dinner speaker should *welcome* a chain reaction of yawns at his lecture. It means that his audience is doing its best to stay awake, instead of simply dozing off. The listeners are sending great quantities of oxygen to their brains which helps them to focus on the lecture (when they yawn).

Watch the cat, when she awakes from a nap. She yawns and stretches to the tip of each paw, before she goes off on the next adventure. She knows instinctively what men have to re-learn, namely, that everything that we do must spring from our creative center, in order to be whole.

"Our bodies are weights, weights moved by energy," Opal Gilpatrick said. Yes, but they are not dead weights. The primary requirement is that they should be fully energized yet "rested" i.e. free of undue tensions, matched to the particular job in hand and timed so that everything works together. The children in Mrs. Russell's class, years ago, called this feeling of resilience and balance having a Light Weight Body. The use of this feeling of resilience should be maintained with every breath we draw, only that man has been too busy, perhaps adjusting to the ever-present machine, to keep the ease that he inherited from his evolutionary forebears. The up-keep of this Light Weight Body breathing is achieved by allowing a "once-further" lateral feeling of extension at the end of your inhalation, before you exhale and a "once-further", vertical exhalation release to float you over to the next inhalation again. It is amazing how much this simple practice will calm and ease your breathing, giving you increased vitality as well.

Everything that we do has a predominant body focus; either a lateral or a vertical extension. All day long we are changing from one extension to the other. Motion forward, up and out will require a lateral extension; a wide feeling, like imaginary wings spread to carry you up or forward. On the other hand if you are skating or dancing backward, there must be a vertical, tall feeling. Try going downstairs and observe how svelte and comfortable you feel, if you exhale and think tall (vertical) as you start.

Sitting down on a low chair, also becomes easy and graceful with a vertical extension to lower you, as if your body were being let down by an invisible cord. If you sit down in a wide, lateral extension, you will surely sprawl, perhaps even endangering the chair springs by the thud of your descent.

A lateral or vertical focus of attention applies as well to our body balances for output and intake. If you speak, there must be a wide feeling, which includes your audience; otherwise you will be simply talking to yourself. When you listen, on the other hand, you must assume a vertical, attentive extension to allow the speakers words to come in; otherwise you will not really hear him, you will be too busy planing your reply. A little practice with the use of lateral and vertical balances will be a great satisfaction, because it makes everything we do much easier.

End results and finished performance have been an obsession, in much of our education, so that the process and the experience of growth have too often been neglected. Even in physical education, competition has been so overdone that there is little enjoyment of a good game; winning is the only thing that counts. We even speak of a game as a *fight*. We have used our bodies as tools to attain our ends, instead of using them as a *means* of savoring life from moment to moment. As Alan Watts says in *The Wisdom of Insecurity*,[1] "The mystery of life is not a *problem to be solved, but a reality to be experienced.*" Creative Motion is a way of deepening our experience of living and offers us satisfaction in the simple things of everyday life as well as in our moments of high achievement.

Before discussing the specific application of Creative Motion to the teaching of music, we turn to Martha Russell's own words:

---

1. The Wisdom of Insecurity, Alan Watts p. 102 *Pantheon Books*

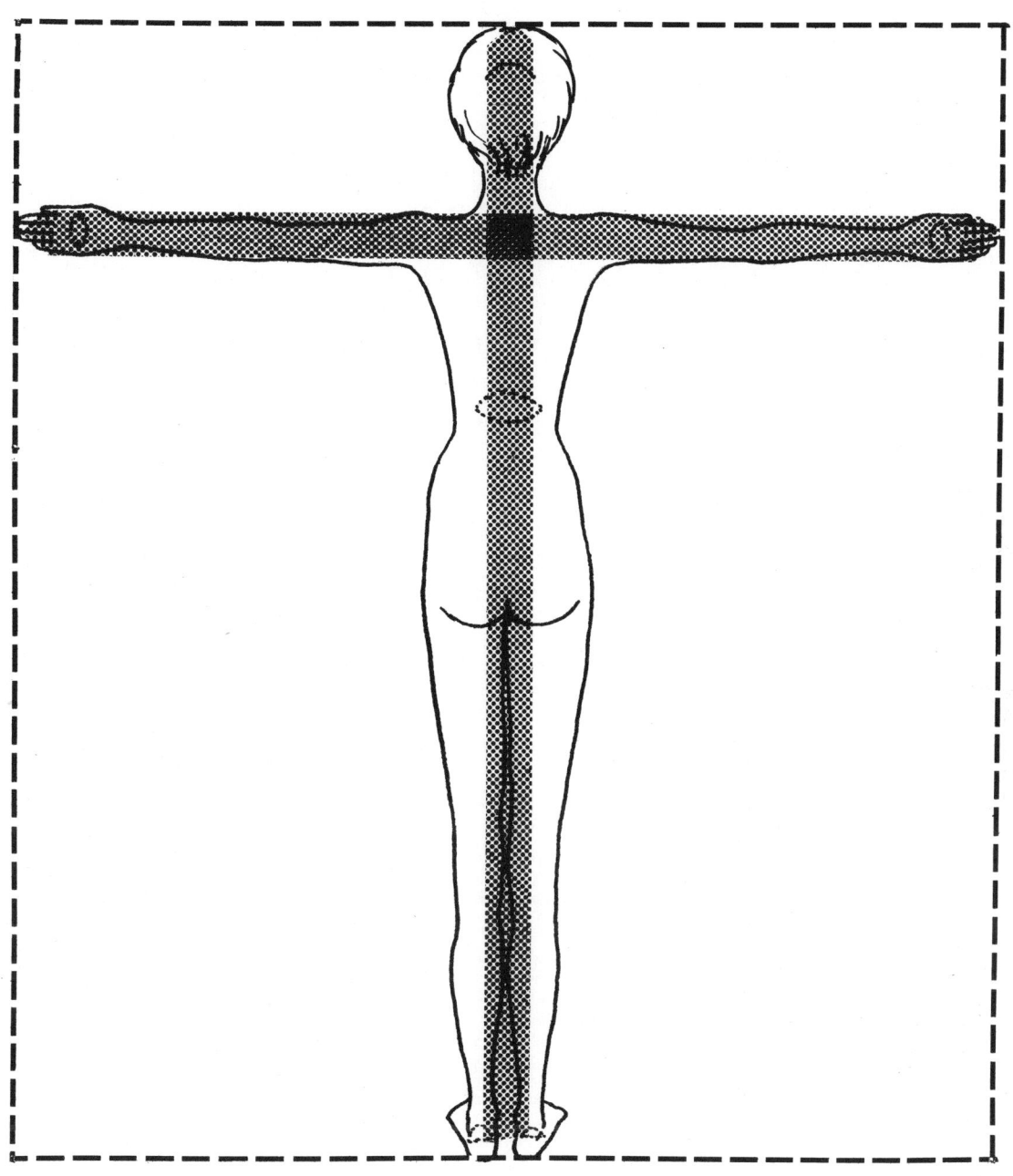

Lateral and Vertical Lines.

FOUR EXERCISES WHICH BACKGROUND BOTH BODY EXPERIENCE & MUSICAL EXPRESSION

Martha S. Russell

These exercises over a period of years and in the order in which they appear here, have been used to make clear:

1. The difference between lung breathing and energy breathing. i.e. lung respiration and energy respiration — the "Ah" breath.
2. What it is that initiates the energy respiration and the body mechanism that handles it — the yawn.
3. A simple method of achieving a Light Weight Body.
4. The two aspects or strands of creative energy in their body relationship, and the way in which they operate to produce *timing* — i.e. *energy control* — in outer action.

THE AH BREATH

1

Take a breath as if you were about to say "Ah", and don't say it. Exhale your lung breath, but keep in your body the energy gearing the exercise gave you. Do this several times until the distinction between lung breath and energy breath i.e. body respiration and energy respiration is clear. Do it again and note what happens at the center of your body when you take a breath as-if-about-to-say-"Ah". Repeat the exercise until you can define for yourself the *feeling* of what happens at the center of your diaphragm when you take an "Ah" breath. Continue the practice of the exercise until you can produce that *happening* at the diaphragmatic center at will.

THE YAWN

2

The analysis of the yawn: a slow movie of respiration, showing the functional relationship of the two aspects or strands of energy in the body.

A - Yawn, and discover for yourself what initiates the yawn (the same happening at the center of the diaphragm). Yawn again and discover for yourself what happens in response to that happening at the diaphragmatic center. Some form of energy is released from the center to the edges of the body. We shall call this energy "radiant energy", until science gives us a name for it. Its action is instantaneous, the way a room lights when you snap on an electric light. We speak of this action of radiant energy as "covering". The body then stretches and unfolds until it reaches the furthest edge that the radiant energy covered instantaneously.

B - Yawn once more and discover for yourself what happens when the inner "motion" of radiant energy and the outer movement of the body meet at the periphery. A second "happening" occurs at the center; there is a "once further" extension of energy and body, a "lift over the top" which reverses the direction of the energy current, and expiration sets in. The radiant energy returns instantly to the center; the body "follows up" in timed relaxation of body breath and muscular energy. It is the exercise which should be used to give you personal and incontrovertible knowledge of the way in which the inner motion strand of (energy) and the outer strand, or body movement respond to ones "governing idea". This response is fundamental to the study of MUSIC and must be clearly understood and under control. We can chart the slow moving picture of respiration, the yawn, as follows:

IMPULSE

A spring at the center of the diaphragm (common to both inner motion and outer movement) starts the inspiration. After this initial impulse the two energy strands, inner motion and outer movement, proceed at different rates.

RADIANT ENERGY – MOTION
Instantaneous *cover* from the center to the focal point of action covered by the governing idea.

BODY ENERGY – MOVEMENT
The body unfolds and stretches in a timed follow up to the extreme point *covered* by the radiant energy.

CLIMAX

When the movement catches up with the motion at the focal point of action, we have reached the climax of the yawn. The spring at the center of the diaphragm automatically repeats itself; there is a "once further" extension of energy which resolves itself into a lift over the top, with a reversal of the direction of the energy current, and expiration sets in. Again, after the initial release over the top, the motion and the movement proceed at different rates.

RADIANT ENERGY – MOTION
Instantaneous return from periphery to center.

BODY MOVEMENT
A follow up of the body in a timed release of breath and muscular energy.

LIGHT WEIGHT BODY
3

The following exercise which has been used to give us conscious experience of the spring at the center of the diaphragm is, possibly, the most foolproof of them all. It adds the knowledge of a basic law in the energy-body equation, which has not yet been brought to our attention, and on which our study of MUSIC is based. This is the exercise you will probably use for daily practice.

Attaining a Light Weight Body.
- A- Stand, exhale, then as your breath comes in, feel your back widen and let your arms float up and out to either side. Take maximum extension through arches of hands and finger tips.
- B- Let your body adjust comfortably over the arches of your feet. Keep arms extended, but do not hold your breath; breathe normally in and out.
- C- When arms begin to get tired, exhale, *letting go the feeling* that is holding up your arms. Your arms will float down to their usual position at your sides, with a feeling of definite timing.

Notice the feeling of "power resting up"; your head free, body comfortably rested down; this gives a vertical two-way stretch; a radiantly coordinated body that is in balance from top to toe. Relax your outer physical body *entirely* letting it rest on, and adjust to, the Light Weight Body in every part. If you can observe yourself in a mirror you will see that your body posture is the best radiantly-coordinated set-up that it could be at the given moment. It will grow better and better as you pursue the exercise – which you will accustom yourself to do every morning on arising. Do this exercise (here and now) over and over, until you can distinguish the feeling of difference in polarization in the Light Weight or heavy weight body. When this is clear, define for yourself the route taken by the energy wave when you rest your power up. Does it feel as if it went, from your arm to your head, outside of your body? No. It seems to return to the center of your body in order to "rest up". It goes instantly. What effects the release and direction of the energy-body configuration? THE SPRING AT THE CENTER OF THE DIAPHRAGM (Ah breath) is the answer to this last question.

TIMING

4

To implement the foregoing: "Make the Gesture with the Diaphragm." Effortless, efficient and beautiful action is "timed" action. The spring at the center of the diaphragm releases the radiant energy that times the action. It would appear that the spring on the diaphragm is the end result of the "inner working" indicated in the definition of "Motion". It is evidently meant to respond instantaneously and automatically to our will-to-act, gearing the body and setting the energy pattern for the action and it seems to be used instinctively, by every created thing in our world, except our selves. Man has out-stripped its instinctive use, and has not yet become aware of it at the conscious level. This conscious awareness must come before the automatic response of "the inner working" to the "governing idea" is assured. The feeling is one of springing at the center of your diaphragm as a swimmer springs on a diving board, down, up, over, onto the object of the action. Only, while the diving board spring is like a slow moving picture, the diaphragm spring is done in a flashing instant. As in the yawn the whole body is alight and geared for action in that instant and, in some curious way, you will seem to have covered the distance and reached the object *before* you start the action. *It is at the moment of starting the physical action that you rest your body down.* Note that this is the same process that we analysed in "the yawn" except that this time the focal point of the action is outside of the body instead of at the body periphery, which often brings about a delayed body-resting-down reaction. Compare each step of the two processes and see that the *yawn is actually a slow moving picture of energy respiration wherever you find it.* In making the gesture of the diaphragm there is no forward movement of the front of the body no tensing or lifting for action. With the initial spring the front of the body relaxes entirely, something (remindful of the action of a camera shutter) seems to open in the back, and *instantly* the entire body is vitalized and tuned to output. This back-thrust of energy apparently registers the energy-compensation for the outgoing action. Acquaint yourself with the feeling of this energy-compensation and do not act unless it is there. *Never* force the action with the *front* of your body. It is the back-thrust and lift of the energy-compensation (rebound) that produces effortless timed action.

Practice this gesture of the diaphragm on a succession of daily tasks for at least five minutes each day; until the automatic response to your intent to act is that instantaneous spring at the diaphragmatic center and the setting of the energy pattern which times the action.

And now we should be ready to Experience MUSIC.

WINDSWEPT

The Workshop Clarion

The Kitchen Crew Starts The Day

WINDSWEPT, The Center Of the Workshop's Activity and Growth

OPAL

All Instruments Are Part Of *Creative Motion* Learning.

CHANTICLEER – The First House To Greet You.

OFFSPRING — One Of The Eight Hand-Made Cabins Tucked In The Woods.

Gathering Lillies For A Terrace Supper.

PART TWO

APPLYING CREATIVE MOTION TO THE TEACHING OF MUSIC
Margaret Allen

Creative motion learning works with universal principles regardless of the level at which we focus our attention. The same principles hold sway from the largest musical entity to the smallest, varying only in size, not in organizational content. Every composition, every movement of a symphony, every phrase, every tone (or rest, for that matter) will be identical in structure. "Motion is the inner working of a governing idea:" the mind-picture of the experience flashed whole, the release of energy, the redirecting of the energy flight to the place or moment in time to which the governing idea has directed it, and the final release of the remaining energy for its return to center to await another governing idea. This is the pathway of Creative Motion as well as the pathway of energy.

The body becomes the physical expression of these various parts which make up the whole. It is the whole self which allows these to be realized in the objective world of tonal and rhythmic motion. If the body is to fulfill its responsibilities as the medium between the governing idea and the musical demands, let us seek aids which will help to bring about this fulfillment.

The laws of motion are not man-created, they are the inevitable result of forces far beyond our power to change. But through our own physical experience we can test and prove these laws; we can live within their sphere of influence, accepting them, using them, honoring them. As one professor said in introducing Creative Motion to a university Music Workshop: "We shall examine principles that we believe are followed intuitively by the talented student, neglected by or unknown to the majority of pupils, but readily available to all. We believe the approach is an unusual one, the results of which may make a significant change in your teaching."

It is energy and our relation to it, and its relation to us, that we are searching for. It is only by experience that we will know the answers. But we do know that where Creative Motion has touched a tone, a melody line, a life, some power has made each one of these, varied as they are, more radiant and more enduring.

CREATIVE MOTION

Energy is the capacity to perform work.
Energy is never lost; it is either transferred or released.

Two forms of energy are involved in any motion:
1. Stored energy called potential,
2. The release of this stored energy called kinetic.

THE UNIVERSAL PRINCIPLE

POTENTIAL
stored energy

KINETIC
the energy of motion

CHART 1

The back and forth are always of equal proportions. No matter how much you use of potential energy, the same amount is given the body in motion.

The Creative Motion Principle

"MOTION IS THE INNER WORKING OF A GOVERNING IDEA."
(Funk and Wagnall unabridged dictionary 1925)

The governing idea flashes your energy whole, for whatever you wish to achieve. The more you use a light-weight-body, the more you are free to follow through to fill in the pathway of this energy charge.

Motion that has all of the parts related to the whole is the most efficient expression of energy and is the fulfillment of the "inner working of the governing idea."

The Procedure

1. The governing idea flashes its message to the diaphragm, the diaphragm sends the message to the hand-arch by way of radiant coordination, the hand-arch moves the fingers as the governing idea has directed.

MIND⟶DIAPHRAGM⟶HAND-ARCH⟶FINGERS

1. The finger drops into the keybed because of the energy output of the person playing. The key-drop expresses directional force. The terms "resting down" and "finger drop" mean an energy thrust with its instantaneous rebound. When we say "resting on motion" we infer that it feels as if the "resting down" and the rebound interlap. Actually the "motion" comes out of the "resting".

2. The energy rebound redirects the energy that has been released because of the oppositional force created by the resistance of the keybed to the finger drop. This redirected energy follows through on an energy flight to complete the action upon which the governing idea focused.

3. The release of energy with its rebound and the flight to the climax cannot be expressed as a whole timed action unless it takes place through the medium of a light-weight-body.

Perhaps it would be helpful to explain the scientific and practical aspects of realizing this light-weight-body by the following diagram and explanation.

A Light-Weight-Body

"Forces always work in pairs of opposites. One force is equal and opposite to the other force."
In any body four forces are at work:

A. TWO FORCES ACTING ON ME
1. Gravity pulling me downward toward the earth's center. (Gravity always seeks its "center of gravity"; in the human body it is the diaphragm.)
2. The earth thrusting me upward. (These are not opposing forces since they both come from the earth's center of power. They are only opposite in direction.)

B. TWO FORCES ACTING ON THE EARTH
1. My body exerting a pull upon the earth. (This is equal and opposite to the gravitational force, but imperceptible because of the relative size of the earth compared with a man or with me.*
2. My body weight pushing down on the earth.

Items A-1 (the gravitational pull on me) and

B-1 (my body's pull upon the earth, which is the levitational force) are an equal and opposite pair, producing balanced opposition at my center of gravity, the diaphragm.

Items A-2 (the earth's thrust pushing me upward) and

B-2 (my body weight pushing down on the earth) are an equal and opposite pair, producing balanced opposition.

The interaction of these natural forces creates a state of being in which we live and move.

How can we use these forces in conjunction with our own energy in order to create a

---

* We expend energy in order to become the oppositional force of gravity.

light-weight-body?

A light-weight-body is one in which the gravitational and levitational forces are in balance at the diaphragmatic center. This is a tonicity body in which all of the parts are related to the whole.

Exercise:
1. Stand at ease with your feet feeling an intimate contact with the earth, as you rest your shoulders down on the rib cage.
2. Exhale. As you let your breath in, feel yourself lifting up from the earth through the arches of your feet.
3. The motion continues up against your back and over the top of your head, coming to rest at your diaphragm (remember, shoulders rested down).

This will give you a light-weight-body, effortless, efficient and radiant. Experience this many times a day. It takes only the time of one breath. It quickly becomes the body you choose to live with. It not only helps you physically, but it gives you a feeling of cosmic relationship with the earth, which is good.

THE INSTRUMENT

Here we are investigating new lines of approach to music training to amplify and enrich our capacity as teachers, to grow that we may help others grow. For the ultimate responsibility of teaching is to learn how to relate, to desire development and to be willing to change. Perhaps the most helpful way to set sail is to consider two definitions of the word "instrument" from Webster's unabridged dictionary (1957).

1. "An instrument is any mechanical contrivance for yielding musical sounds, as an organ, piano, flute or violin."

Here we have an instrument that possesses no active thought or power of will; a contrivance which yields musical sounds only when an external force is added. The creative work is done on the instrument, not by the instrument. It takes a mind and a heart to create. A piano, a violin, an organ or a flute possesses no such ability of its own; it only "yields its sounds"; the possibility of yielding music must be created for it.

2. "An instrument is the means or medium used to accomplish a purpose."

To accomplish a purpose is to seek a goal, to work toward a desired end. In this definition the instrument is a motivating, living being; one with the power of choice by way of understanding and desire who must provide the musical necessities so that those otherwise silent instruments can yield their tonal beauty.

The first random hitting of the keys by a toddling child can generate the "musical sound", but not even a doting parent would consider these tones a claim to music. What is lacking if sound is there? Why isn't it music? It is not music until the sounds are inter-related with more than just sequence. They must be bound together by inner dynamic forces which relate them in fascinating ways. It is these relationships that give power and tension, meaning and movement. Becoming aware of these relationships is the "purpose to be accomplished." Only the most remote chance would make the hit-or-miss sounds of the three-year-old create relationships necessary to give musical meaning. The power of choice, the sensitivity to feel, these are the characteristics of this living instrument.

How many teachers have advertised themselves as "Piano Teachers", forgetting that a piano can learn nothing? We are not trying to teach a piano with its eighty-eight keys in juxtaposition; rather we are helping to make the student and ourselves sensitive to the inner demands of the music and our relationship to them. These chosen alternatives are a thousand times more exciting. A human being, "the medium to accomplish a purpose," contrasts sharply with a "mechanical contrivance constructed for yielding musical sounds." Yet both are necessary to musical study. The human instrument, however, should always come first in our concern.

In the art of singing or the dance the involvement of two distinct instruments does not occur. Here the means or medium for yielding the tone or providing the rhythmic tensions are one with the instrument to "accomplish a purpose." Both are united. The whole body is called upon to express these arts. Lotte Lehman once said, "You sing with every cell in your body," and who would think of a Nijinsky dancing with only his feet in motion? Every tone, every rhythmic tension, every nuance is the expression of a whole; the free-play of the inner to the outer, the center radiating to the periphery.

In the instance of the piano as an instrument, the complete keyboard is laid out clearly before us. We may not fathom it, but we see it waiting to be played. The living instrument, however, is likely to remain in more hidden recesses. The imagination, the will-to-do, the body flexibility, the inherent love of motion, these characteristics are not immediately evident nor easily accessible. But they form the living instrument, the sum total of each individual: his ear, his eye, his neuro-muscular organism on the physical side; his sensitivity, his acceptability, his wonder, his inner aliveness on the personality side. For a precious time these qualities are at our disposal as teachers (if we are aware of them) to be sympathetic toward, to nurture and to enjoy.

But perhaps the most important lesson of all is that which dancing and singing gives to the world: the necessity to be whole; to unite the two instruments; to transcend their differences; and, above all, to let music live through us by our complete acceptance of its demands.

THE EAR APPROACH

Let us start our music training with the ear. I suggest this as a beginning because music is the art of sound, an aural art. It is a hearing-feeling synchronism, one in which the ear serves as a pathway into the intimate world of tone. Would anyone start to paint a landscape with his eyes blindfolded? Or to dance a waltz with his body bound? Certainly we should start music with the ear. Beside this, ear sensitivity begins at the center of a child's awareness, and to start at the center is our main objective. As one little first grader said: "I see with the front of my face, but I hear with the back of my head."

If real growth starts at the center, and if a child hears music as something "way off in the back of his head" (certainly a center concept), perhaps that is the reason music gets such immediate response from a child, more so than any other "tool of attention." The teacher does not need to say again and again, "Quiet children, please." All she needs to do is to play the first phrase of Beethoven's Fifth Symphony and suddenly the extraverted motion is magically changed to quiet. As Sylvia Ashton-Warner says in her book *Teacher,* "It is not just silence, but stillness; every eye on me; every hand poised; an intensity of stillness born of sound." My grandchild, just over the edge of one year, will stop crying if I sing as little as one phrase of a song. It is as if I spoke a musical language that she could translate in a flash of time, a language that she did not need to learn for it was her living birthright.

What does happen when one hears music? It almost seems as if there were two sets of ears responsive to the musical phenomenon. First, the outside ear relates to the air vibrations. It catches them on the wing to sort out and to arrange into aural images.

Second, the inner ear instantaneously captures the outside ear's tonal experience and holds it centered to re-hear, re-evaluate and to re-sing. The tones flood and undulate; they fill the mind with tonal color. The inside ear becomes the reflection on the pool of the mind of all that the outer ear has heard.

My first suggestion is to let the teacher play for the student (of any age) a simple melody that she has previously created. I say this with careful consideration of the teacher's need to relate. A lesson that has been thought through, planned through, lived through is inevitably far superior to one that has been approached without creative effort. Great teaching does not just happen. A good teacher works at teaching before a lesson ever starts. She protects and nourishes her responsibilities. It is a frame of mind that disciplines and anticipates. I once asked a doctor why he had been so successful with his patients. He waited for his answer, and then said, "I always say a short prayer before I walk into my patient's room. I never just go in." A teacher has as much at stake as a doctor. The doctor is bound to the whole of a person, but so are we. The only difference is that our channel is that of music.

"But what makes a melody?" you ask. "How do various notes become a good melody or remain a poor one?"

The journey of a melody, exclusive of atonal music, is much like the kind of journey you would like to take yourself, a going away, an experience in a new place, and a return. It is a melodic blueprint of almost any kind of activity, of life itself. So if we are to translate this journey into tone all we basically need to know is the "home" tone 1, two other arrival tones 3 and 5 that can be used in place of 1 (3 is gentle and loving, 5 is aggressive and strong), the going away, tension tones, 2 and 7, that are also very anxious to return, and the weaker tones, 4 and 6, which almost always go down to their next door neighbor for their eventual arrival.

We call this tonal dynamics: the relationship of tones in a magnetic field of force. Tones within a musical context have a further significance beyond their individual pitch. They are bound by some inner urgency to respond to the magnetic pull of the center tone of 1. They do not always answer the command immediately. Holding off their arrival is one of the functions of music. This adds tension and drama to the musical scene. But in the end the command is almost always obeyed, ending on either 1, 3 or 5. The tones also express individual relations to each other (e.g. 4 goes to 3, 6 goes to 5).

Instead of using the Italian syllables, do, re, mi, which have no dynamic significance, we will use the same number symbols as the eight notes of the octave. Sing and sing these tonal relations. Stand with the body balanced slightly forward. Let your hand follow the curves of tonal tendency rather than just "placing a tone in mid air." It is easy to get the body involved. An action tone such as 5 projects a forward feeling with an active body response quite naturally and unselfconsciously. The 4 and 6 are, as it were, "behind the line," and have not the tonal strength to return to 1. They make the easiest possible shift: 4 goes down a half step to 3, 6 accepts 5 for an arrival. The body balance in response to these two less urgent tones is behind center, the weight balance is on the heels rather than the arch of the foot. As one boy said, "4 and 6 are like standing behind the pasture gate ready to climb over onto the horse's back standing close by." (3 and 5)

It is not for the teacher to tell pupils what to do. She suggests it inarticulately with her own body response as she sings with them. Her responsibility is to give them a chance to hear and to find out for themselves the meaning of tonal motion. Soon many of them will hear the pull of the 1 as a tone of equilibrium as well as the urgency of other tonal relationships almost as easily as they hear pitch. The great requisite is that one listens and responds with his whole self.

Very soon you can begin to play tunes such as "Hot Cross Buns" or "Frere Jacques" and let the students either sing them, using the tonal dynamic symbols, or play them on the piano in response to the hearing. Or better still, create melodies, simple ones with few intervals for the students to relay. Have them create melodies too, hear-feel the melody first with inside singing, so the tunes will not be slow and ponderous. It is not just "the note", rather "the going" that is important; the dynamic motion, the pull of the tones we must hear.

It really helps to make music alive from the very first.

TONAL DYNAMIC CHART

Settle down on this tone: sing "one, one, one" etc. As you sing spring your hand on the diaphragm level. Feel tall and wide at the same time.

Feel 2 being pulled back to 1. It sounds like the undertow feels as the receding wave pulls at your ankles.

3 could be happy staying on 3. It feels quite secure where it is, but also enjoys returning to 1.

4 is a weak tone. It does not venture very far from home. 3 being close, and a good secure neighbor, it just goes to 3.

5 is very full of action. It likes to go anywhere. Sometimes it obeys the pull of 1, or it remains on 5.

And now look at 5. It has found a new place to go, just as good as 1, in fact it sounds like 1 but higher. It has the same dynamic power as 1.

6 is another note like 4. It does not feel like going so far as 1. Instead it feels the pull of 5. So 6 goes to 5.

7 is the most eager of all the tones. It goes immediately to 8 if no other tones interrupt the going. 1 is so far away the dynamic power of 1 has been transferred to 8 which sounds the same as 1 an octave higher.

Creative Motion Highlights*

    Feeling the motion should come out of the aural image. Hearing grows out of motion.
    Music is something we have to put through our bodies to hear.
    You can go no further than experience takes you.
    You will know only that which you have experienced, not that which you have been told.
    To sing one needs to have a body that can extravert the inside knowing.
    To sing one must become one with the music.

* Quotations taken from Martha Russell and Opal Gilpatrick.

THE EYE APPROACH

The bridge from ear to eye is one in which the listened-to tones become materialized as notes on the staff. To the ear, a note is a particular tone; to the eye, a note is a particular place.

The pupil and teacher who have worked through the previous chapter, however, know more than just a "particular tone." The tone by itself is not the important thing. One tone is only the promise of music. It has nothing to relate to, so it has no real value, no musical meaning. The pupil and teacher began to hear and feel the relationship of one tone to another, an inner tension, a leaning toward, an arrival. They not only heard and felt, but they identified with the tonal tendencies by letting their bodies inform them of the tonal qualities. It is a forward hearing, like listening to a magnetic field of force, the tones seemingly are being moved for or against their wills. The dynamic quality is the motion of inner tension and will-to-move, and gives tones their musical meaning. We carried the idea of motion no further than that — no metre, no rhythmic duration. We will take this single-minded route suggested by the ear approach and consider only pitch, direction and interval for the eye approach.

To the eye, as we have said, "a note is a particular place." The first and most experiential way to fulfill this definition is to draw notes on the staff, singing the tonal dynamic number with each note drawn. Drawing notes and intervals on the staff, each in its particular place, is a more exacting experience than playing a note someone else has drawn or printed. Note-drawing is a tidy discipline; there is no guessing leeway. Furthermore, only the eye is responsible.

Adjacent notes need little consideration, for there is no mistaking where they go — "right next" as the children say. The hazard is the interval, the "space between." Here is the inevitable moment of doubt and hesitation. Becoming alerted to the various sized intervals is the important thing for the eye to accomplish.

The simplest interval group is that of the triad 1-3-5. The teacher will put down the piano ledge and ask the pupil to place the 1-5 position down on the ledge with the thumb and fifth finger supporting the arch, singing the tones 1-5 as he does so. Within that hand position of 1-5, drop down the third finger, singing the tone of the third. Let us see what we have. Three fingers down with an unused finger between each of the supporting fingers. To match this with the notes on the staff, there will be an interval between 1 and 3, and 3 and 5. If 1 is on a line, 3 and 5 will be on the next two lines respectively, with a space between each. Draw the triad starting it on each line of the staff. The triad on the fourth and fifth lines will use ledger lines, which is good for it allows early acquaintance with "off-staff" reading.

Transferring the triad onto the spaces is readily accepted, for the logic of position is the same for both lines and spaces. If 1 is on a space, 3 and 5 will also be on a space. The same inclusive training used on the lines can be used for the spaces. The interval of a 7th can be added to the notation after the triad has been firmly fixed by repeated note-drawing. Since this interval often lies outside of a child's hand-arch span, the 7th must not be included in a hand position if this is the case.

INTERVAL ON LINES — 3rd — one space between each line bearing note.
        5th — two spaces between each line bearing note.
        7th — three spaces between each line bearing note.

INTERVAL ON SPACES — 3rd — one line between each space bearing note.
        5th — two lines between each space bearing note.
        7th — three lines between each space bearing note.

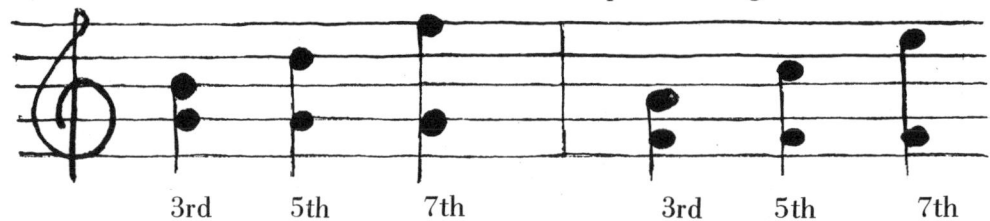

The interval of a 4th, 6th and 8th (or octave) having a wider tonal spread, the unit is "line-space" or "space-line" depending upon the first note of the interval. The interval of a 6th doubles the original unit, the 8th triples it. If the lower note of the interval of a 4th, 6th, or 8th is placed on a line, the top note will be on a space, and *vice versa*. Thus they are easy to distinguish from the interval of a 3rd, 5th, 7th.

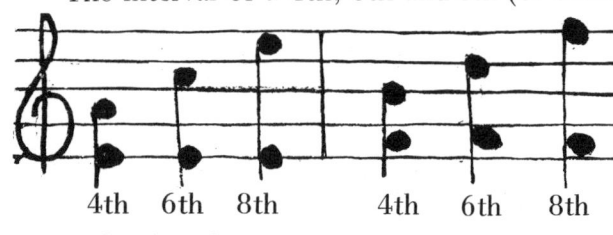

The intervals of a 4th and 6th are harder to sing, even by a student whose musical training extends over years. Perhaps it is because we are intuitively sentient to the over-tone series which anticipates the basic triad. Whatever the reason, it is necessary to become familiar with these intervals — their look, their sound, their hand-shape. Sing them, draw them, shape them in the hand. Do it again and again, starting on different places so your eye spots them anywhere on the staff. One or two ledger lines above and below the staves should be included. They help to relate the clefs in addition to widening the tonal area.

After the interval of a 4th and 6th have been secured in singing and drawing, let the top tone of the 4th resolve to the 3rd, and the top tone of the 6th resolve to the 5th according to their dynamic tendencies. To support actual note reading with the "hear-feel" understanding of tonal dynamics greatly increases reading rapidity and adds the musical quality which is the desire of every serious pianist.

Reading music should not be a trial and error process, but an exact knowing. The time spent on intervals is the clue. There is far more fun and satisfaction in reading music if this preliminary training has been carried out. Of course the names of the lines and spaces must be memorized along with their key equivalents, but that too is more quickly learned if the name of both lines and spaces stems from one related idea. "All cows eat grass" is one mental image, but it suffices for four particular spaces and is far easier to remember.

It is a three way relayed message: singing the interval, drawing the notes on the staff, getting an immediate hand response to cover the interval size. In this way the child creates everything: the singing tones, the note picture and the hand shape. Not even the piano helps in the process. The child is the whole instrument.

If the student burns with that initial fire to be given a "song to play," why not write out several in his notebook illustrating directional lines and intervals? Help him to discover the note relationships which lead to musical understanding through the eye.

TROT, TROT, TROT

Example: TROT, TROT, TROT
  Before the reading is put into tone, it is most helpful for the student to discover what makes the song move.
  Intervals 1-3-5 up, using lines
  Scale pattern down using all five fingers
  Intervals 1-3-5 down, using spaces
  Intervals 1-3-5 down, using lines.
  Intervals 1-3-5 down, using spaces
  Intervals 1-3-5 down, using lines
  Scale pattern up, all five fingers
  Scale pattern down, all five fingers.

Example: SWINGING HIGH, SWINGING LOW
 Here the scale patterns are so simple that only the intervals need attention. The intervals are more varied. Name the intervals, or write their shape on the score before you play them.
 Up a 5th, down a 4th, up a 5th, down a 5th, up a 6th, down a 3rd, up a 5th, repeat
 Final octave interval in both hands. The motion is carried *by the hand arch* on all intervals, never by the fingers.

NOTE VALUE TIMING

Man has always loved to move with music, not because he wills to move, but because he cannot help but move. It is an instinctive urge that has no boundaries of place or people. It takes in the whole wide world.

There are many ways that one can move to music: feeling its inner swing and responding to it as it rides the crest of wave after wave; moving with the rhythm of the melody as it free-lances its way into the outer world; springing with the intervals as they search the limits of their vitality (or hover close to a waiting before they again take flight); or experiencing phrase motion as it gradually emerges. Music has them all. They are the sum total of its Being.

To begin with let us start with the rhythm of the melody, "note-value timing" we call it. There is little need for explanation, the music explains in its illimitable way the sound of its motion. Ears hear, the body feels and away the class goes to free the music into extraverted action.

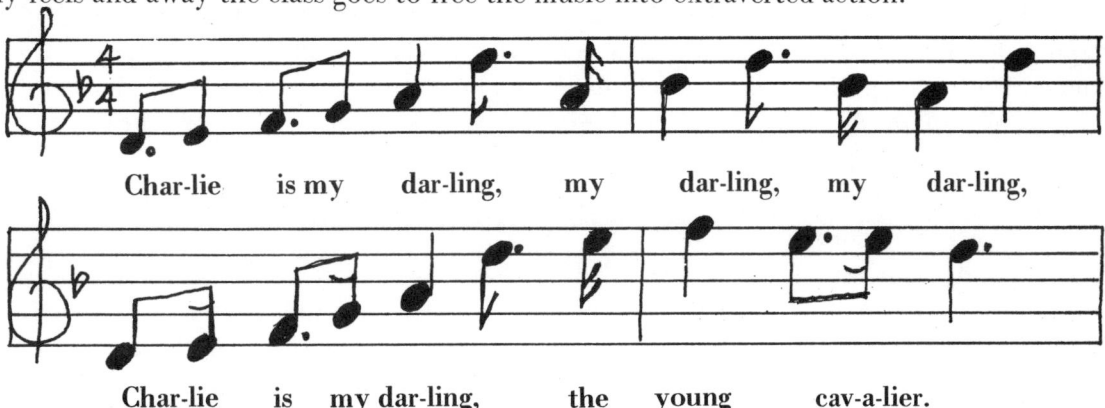

It doesn't take many tries to realize that something unquestionably happens beyond the confines of rhythmic duration if one actively experiences the music. The more a person moves to music, the more he realizes that each individual note-value suggests a particular body response. Skipping notes done with a walking-note body are thick and heavy, like a padded clown at a summer circus; or half notes walked with a sixteenth note body makes one feel as if he were stilted on stork legs; the grace and the control of the slower motion has completely vanished. What is wrong when the body and the music do not merge into one experience? Or better still, what is right when the body and the music move together?

Instead of using "Charlie is my darling" (which is perhaps too exciting to become aware of what actually happens), let us move to one measure each of the basic note-values in order to discover the natural law governing our physical adjustment to different rates of speed:

$$\mathbf{o} \mid \mathbf{\circ} \; \mathbf{\circ} \mid \mathbf{\circ.} \; \mathbf{\bullet} \; \mathbf{\circ.} \; \mathbf{\bullet} \mid \mathbf{\bullet} \; \mathbf{\bullet} \; \mathbf{\bullet} \; \mathbf{\bullet} \mid \mathbf{\text{♫♫♫♫}} \mid \mathbf{\text{♫.♫.}} \; \text{etc.}$$

With our feeling-action sensitivity what do we discover? We sense an anticipation, a liaison between the immediate note we are on and the next one about to be experienced, so that our body balance is in rapport with the rhythmic necessities. We sense the quality of time duration with the related body textures. This is termed *cover* as applied to rhythm. Rhythmic cover is relating forward in order to anticipate an adjustment of power in relation to a change in note-value with its change of corresponding body balance. *Cover* is the specific of the larger and more inclusive word *Timing*: the release of power so that all of the parts are related to the whole. It is both cover and timing that a successful athlete uses in a swift race. Before the gun fires, he does not stand erect with a low body balance, his weight on his whole foot. Rather, he leans forward, balancing his diaphragm over his hands that lightly touch the ground, his weight on the front foot-arch, his body sixteenth note high, ready to spring like a panther. He has *Covered* his take-off. He has *Timed* his race.

The natural law of body balance is this: any change in the speed of one's motion demands a change in the body balance. This change takes place in the middle of the preceding step before the change occurs, (walking to running, running to skipping, etc.). In the middle (or half value) of the last walking step one shifts his body balance in readiness for the following running motion, etc. The faster one goes, the lighter one feels, if his body is obeying the laws of motion. This is due to a shift in body balance. The more perfectly one synchronizes his body to the rate of speed, the more efficient and effortless is the result. This sounds complicated, but we approximate it whenever we change our quality of motion. Watch yourself as you go from walking to running. See how you automatically shift to a higher balance, throwing the body weight onto the ball of the foot rather than using the chain process of heel-arch-ball-toes as in walking.

Everything that moves has a particular relation to its motion. If so, why should not notes have their individual balance point since they are the sound of motion? We, as the medium between the note and its outside world contact, must discover through our physical rhythmic reaction to the music the exact balance for each individual note in order to express the true sound of the rhythmic pattern.

This is actually the meaning of note-value timing: the note symbol, the adjustment of the body to match this symbol, and the sound made manifest.

The same natural law of motion applies as much to movement on the keyboard as to movement in the world at large. Note-values are the quality of time duration with related body textures; they demand the inner adjustment of force to outer balance. The application of the law to inner musical hearing-feeling is of the utmost importance for it makes one become creative. Our hearing-feeling, when sensitively trained, will make the demands. Even group clapping, usually so flat-hard and boring in sound, becomes flexible and "sound-interesting" if the group becomes aware of the note-values related to the body textures. Clapping with a sixteenth-note hand and body balance sounds nothing like clapping produced by quarter-note quality of motion.

The hands must breathe the music, they do not play the piano. You must discover that which happens in your whole body mechanism to create that which your mind wants to hear. Listen to the music sing inside before you play. Your ears become marvelously sensitive to a new quality in music, a quality of tone produced by the union of inner power and outer activity. It is a quality of tone that melds relationships by *covering* a change in body balances to off-set a change in note-values. Even these three notes on the same pitch will each have their own identity of sound as well as their duration, if they are played as we suggest.

If you study the charts below, you will see the placement of body balance in relation to a given note-value. In moving with different rates of motion, try to become aware of the natural relation between the body balance in the legs and its immediate correspondence in the foot. This inter-response is a law of motion, but becoming aware of it increases your use of the law.

As you begin to apply this experience of note-value balances to your compositions, you become sensitive to the placement of a particular note-value in the hand arch with its corresponding finger response. And if you really feel the motion of the music you will take into account the body balance as it adjusts to the various time values of the notes. Unless there is body relationship to the note-values, the total adjustment can never be complete, and the sound of the music will never quite achieve the demands set forth in the composition.

MELODIC BALANCES

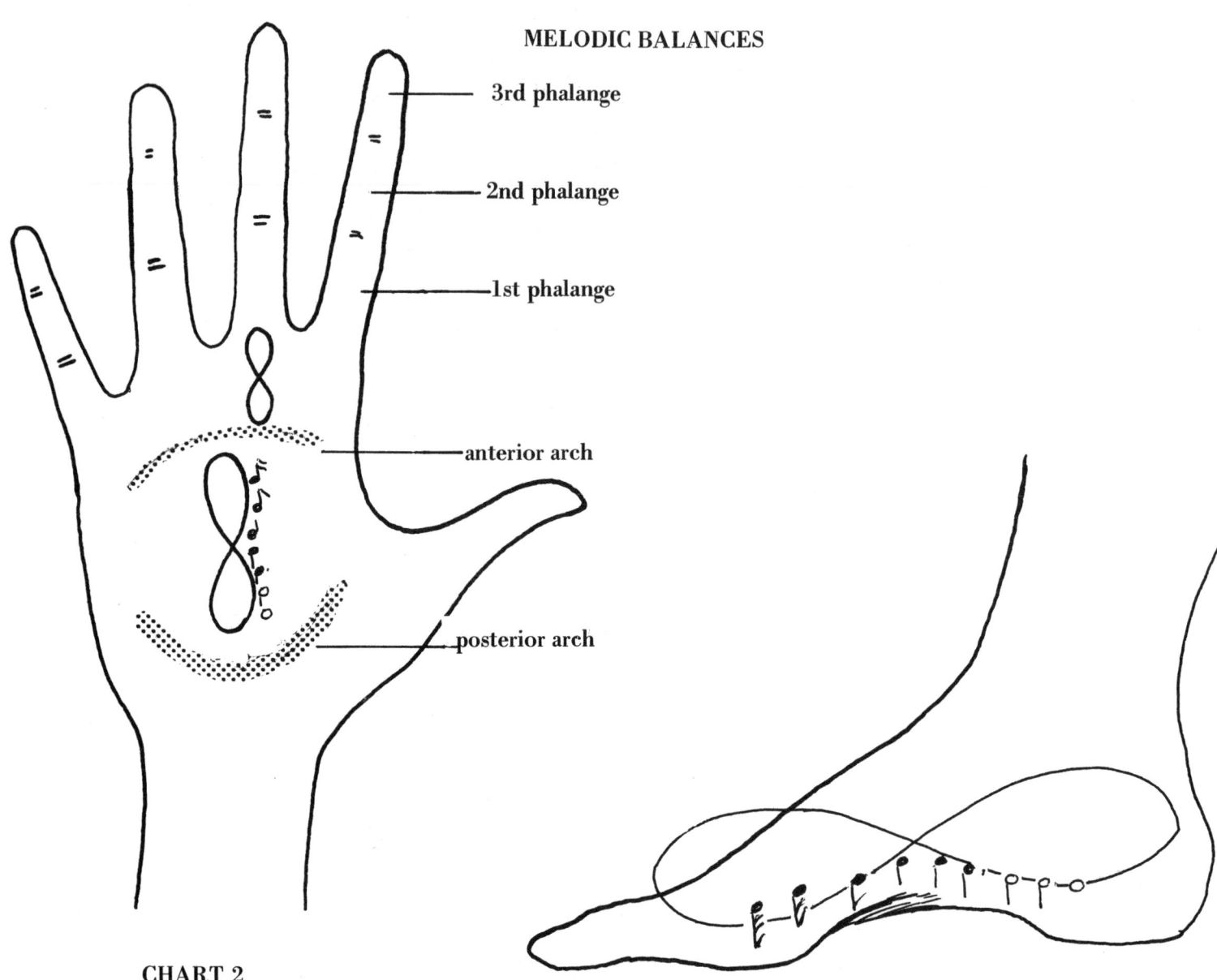

CHART 2

Instead of practising fingers in relation to piano keys (all timed the same way and all sounding the same), your practising must include the hearing-feeling sensitivity which is developed by constant awareness of the inner motion of the music. All scales are included as music. Giving time every day to careful scale practise, with hand balances done in response to various note-values, will serve as a road leading to all music you will ever study. Scales are a technical tool which makes for ease of handling music in relation to its inner motion.

Rest all of yourself on the *going*. Hear the drive; hear the notes fall on the flight of the rebound. Tone is never organized unless the body is over it. Everything in the body rests on the hand-arch. The hand-arch is the plastic part, not the fingers. Never pull away from the keys; this thins the tone and makes for tonal leakage. As long as you are on a note, you must put all of yourself into that experience.

Be sure that the body matches the motion with a "follow-through" feeling, as if it were hanging over the top of the motion. The arch of the hand always leads, never the fingers. You come to the utmost of the arch-spring on every note you play. The spring, as an expression of the rebound in the hand-arch, is the result of the keybed resistance to the finger drop.

The crossing of the thumb is always made through the arch. Keep the arch over the thumb (this eliminates any undue wrist twisting, which bumps the following thumb tone — perilous to scale passages). The thumb immediately "tucks" under, covering the next thumb tone without disturbing the arch position. After the thumb plays, the arch shifts to its new five finger position, keeping itself as level as possible.

Lateral and Vertical Motion

Every complete scale moves in two directions, a going out and a return. All music moves in these two directions. The going up in pitch is the *Lateral Line,* coming down in pitch is the *Vertical.*

Bodily motion easily illustrates these two qualities of direction. Walk forward briskly and sense the wide, broad swathe that your body makes. This is the lateral line of motion. Now walk the same pathway backward. How different it feels; the breadth of the lateral line has completely vanished. A tall up-and-down feeling takes over. This is the vertical line. Inhalation serves the lateral, exhalation the vertical. Try it and see how truly it works that way and what ease it gives to the miracle of breathing.

The word "banking," a term used by aviators, water and snow skiers and other athletes, suggests well the necessary physical adjustment made to change of direction. The skier banks his body around the curve to compensate for the centrifugal force which tends to throw him away from the center. Since the pianist adjusts to change of direction in much the same manner as a body in motion, we use the same terminology. Going up with the right hand, you bank toward the fifth finger side of the hand; coming down in pitch you bank toward the thumb side. In the left the hand banks toward the thumb for its lateral ascent, toward the fifth finger for its vertical descent.

The simple process of breathing exemplifies perfectly the change of direction from lateral to vertical and from vertical to lateral. Let me quote from Mrs. Russell: "Now I always think lateral when I am going to inhale and add 'once further' lateral to release to the vertical feeling of exhalation, and if I do this I keep my center to circumference extension intact and my light-weight-body going."

To make the change of direction an inside-to-outside experience rather than a peripheral gesture, the further extension is absolutely necessary. The climax of a respiration is the "turn-over" from lateral to vertical and will never be realized without the "once further" which makes the climax possible. (In descending scales the climax is on the further extension of the vertical motion.)

Changing direction adds nuance to the tone if the body rides the motion of the "over-the-top" turn. In the scale this nuance adds flexibility and freedom, if it is the natural result of inside to outside response to the extension of lateral and vertical motion.

SUGGESTIONS FOR NOTE-VALUE TRAINING

1. Rest your hand on the table, fingers extended, flat down, body balanced over the hand-arch.
2. As you focus on a particular phalange that corresponds to one of the three note values

♩ ♪ 𝅘𝅥𝅮 , raise and lower the finger in that particular phalange section. You will lift the fingers up by using the muscles between the knuckles. Remember to change your body balance when you change the note-value.

On the Piano

1. Repeat the exercise on the keyboard, playing a measure of ♩♩♩ focused on the first phalange. Your body should be balanced over the interaction section of the knee, the "action" just above the knee, the "feeling" just below the knee. The reason: you do not walk on a sad errand with the same quality of motion used to go to a football game or gay party.

2. Readjust your body to an ♪ balance, followed by a measure of ♪♪♪ focused on the second phalange. See the hand-arch lift slightly as it leans over onto the anterior arch.

3. Now repeat for the 𝅘𝅥𝅮𝅘𝅥𝅮𝅘𝅥𝅮 after you have adjusted your body to match 𝅘𝅥𝅮 . Each measure should have a different sound if you have been sensitive to diaphragm, hand-arch, note-value relations.

Did you notice that the faster the note the closer to the tip of the finger the key contact came?

GENERAL SUGGESTIONS FOR SCALE PRACTICE

Preparation

1. Have a tuned light-weight-body. Back up so you hang over the arches of your feet and stay at that level.

2. Gear for the energy charge covering the whole scale. "See it finished."

3. Hands ready on the keys. Exhale. As your breath comes in, respire the scale up (lateral with inhalation), down (vertical on exhalation).

4. Let go the feeling that holds your hands in readiness.

Playing

1. Let your finger drop into the beginning key, establishing the opposition balance of pressure down and power up.

2. Underneath the light-weight-body feeling in the hands, roll the hands up the keyboard and fall them down the keyboard over the ball bearing feeling in the arch of the hand.

3. Repeat the scale with attention on the lateral expansion on the upward drive and the vertical body release on the downward fall.

4. Repeat again with the attention to the "once further" extension, the force of which turns the direction from the top tone down or from the lowest tone up.

A FOLK SONG WITH NOTE-VALUE ACTION SYMBOLS

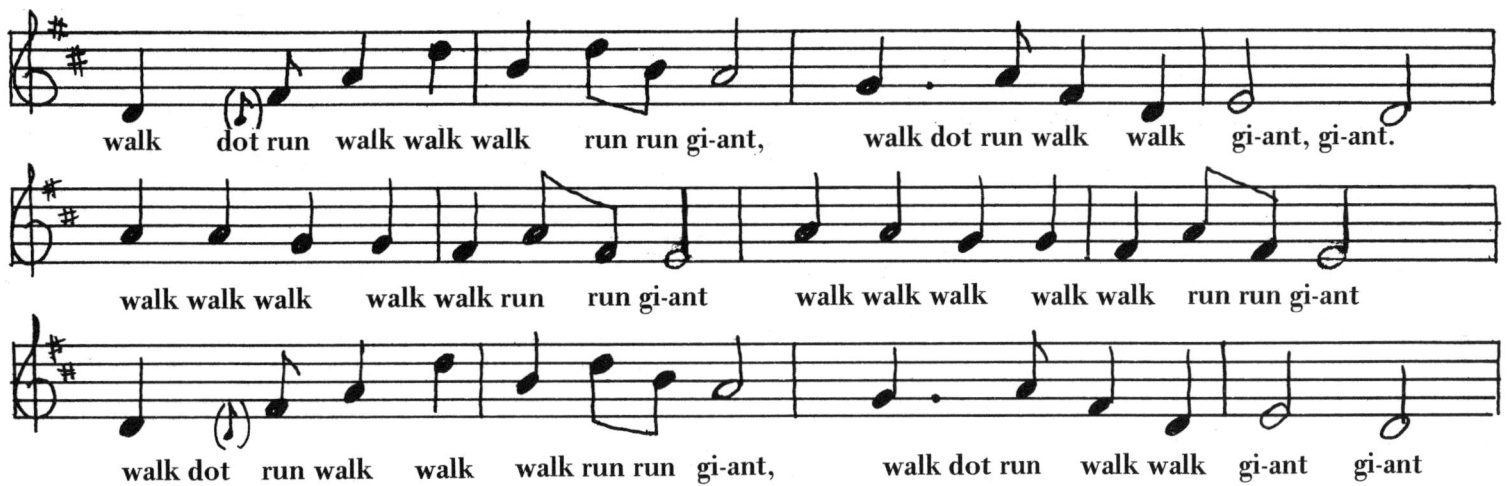

The dot has an eighth note value both in timing and in the body and hand arch balances. You "cover" by changing your balance for it on the last half of the previous quarter note. Played this way the body motion is as smooth as a bird song. Played without rhythmic relationships it is awkwardly disappointing. (Remember that the dot is part of the second beat. This helps to reaffirm the liaison between the dot and the following eighth note.)

Using action words makes the note-values more real. They become a living experience with the body response that includes the hand-arch and fingertips. This sort of training makes one sensitive to the texture of the music. Even the first reading of a song includes a response to the balances contained in the various note-values. This is one of the goals; the student is never outside of the meaning of the music made real by the body-note-value relationship.

Creative Motion Highlights

When you sing music to yourself, you think motion. You must think it in your body.
The body texture matches the level of the music, which is the rhythmic value of the fastest note.
You achieve this body texture before you start to play and maintain it throughout the entire song.
Your body is the physical expression of the flight.
You are whole, so all of you rests on the piano, singing the music.
The power of the motion is started on the first impact with the keys.
The "going" is in the arch, which in turn influences the arm.
The body rides the arch.
Edge and finish come from the head and finger control.
The diaphragm is the place where power is created. It is the interaction center.
The feeling we get from the page creates the sound.
Playing is always the result of your inner readiness.

INTERVALS

Music has always had intervals — the distance between two notes, the space between two beats, sometimes more, sometimes less. Regardless of the size, the psychological meaning of space does not change for it satisfies a basic need in man to express freedom, to convey courage, to exalt exuberance and to honor the zest of life. In studying the use of interval in Western music one begins to realize that music is a "space art" as well as a "time art". Music moves through time, but the choice of rhythmic and tonal interval uses space to fill time's inevitable pulse with further meaning.

We know space only as we recall the physical experience of moving from one place to another; the energy it takes to put space between our steps; to jump, to leap, to feel the excitement of "space between." Can anyone forget the intervals in the opening theme of Brahms' Third Symphony? After the melody makes its dramatic descent, it leaps with that magnificent energy charge from middle C to high A-flat, thirteen scale steps, an insignia of power.

It is not just the wide-scoped interval that portrays to the listener distinct aural images. The smallest interval in our western music, the half step, is a feeling-tool for composers' use. It constricts and intensifies; it clenches with tonal forceps; it embodies bitterness and sorrow or an insecure hovering far more than a larger interval could ever do. Stravinsky in his Symphony of Psalms uses the half step interval superbly to trace the tragic wandering of the ancient tribes of Israel.

Intervals are the relationship of energy demand to interval size. It is this relationship that gives to each interval its particular quality. It is as if the notes were saying, "How much spring must I have to jump from here to there?" But what exactly is our relationship to intervals? How does an interval convey its meaning to us? Here let me quote from *The Composer's World* by Hindemith: "To understand the connection between the movement from tone to tone in music on the one hand and the feeling of special movement on the other, we must find a common denominator of both factors. The equation is: the physical effort which we know is necessary to change from one tone to another equals the physical effort we imagine when we think of a change of position in our common physical experience. It is the relative amount of energy that counts for our evaluation of musical space."*

Keyboard Intervals, however, are deceptive. They look within easy reach so that the individual fingers stretch for them oblivious of arch control. But intervals are achieved by an arch rebound, caused by the reaction of finger pressure to the keybed resistance which releases the energy for the rebound. All finger articulation, rightfully conceived, stems from the hand-arch. The energy out-put, centered in the arch, instantaneously covers the interval and allows the fingers to drop down out of the arch to express their final definition. An interval "stretched and reached for", independent of the arch, will never be a satisfying nor timed interval. At that moment the interval flight is cancelled out; the interval as a measurer of energy is lost sight of; the interval as a feeling experience is forgotten.

* Hindemith, Paul. A COMPOSER'S WORLD. Harvard University Press, Page 52

Thinking intervals, singing intervals, springing intervals prove better than words the real meaning of interval as the child of energy.

Intervals related to diaphragm and foot arch
1. Stand with one foot forward, placing your weight balance on the front foot.
2. Now hear-feel the tone of "one" as a place of equilibrium. As you pulse on the diaphragm and arches of the feet, sing "one, one, one, one."
3. Take a whole step forward with the back foot (which now becomes the front foot) singing "two." The pressure of the step against the floor resistance immediately springs you back to "one."
4. Similarly a rebound will take flight over the interval of a "third" ready to rest on the front foot, with a rebound back to "one."
5. You will realize an increase of energy compensating for size increase as you continue the intervals from 1 to 8. After the interval 1 to 5 your body cannot absorb the increased space of the larger intervals, but you feel an increased energy output.

Now let us consider the half step interval motion:
Return to "one" placing the front foot on a level with the back foot arch.
Pulse back and forth over this half-step interval singing "half-step, half-step" until the feeling of the half-step tension vibrates through your body.

Chart 3 shows the impulse and climax of the interval action, with the energy flight going slightly beyond the second tone so that it can finally come down to rest on the desired climax of the interval.

Chart 4 shows the incorrect way: no rebound, no flight, using finger stretch to cover space which involves only peripheral "untimed" action.

Chart 3 also describes a rule of nature: due to the margin of nature the energy charge always exceeds the space requirement.

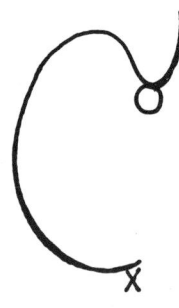 

Chart 3   **Chart 4**

Intervals related to hand-arch
1. Sit or stand according to the class structure. With the elbows flexed let the hands be about level with the diaphragm. Hear-feel the tone of "one." Pulse hand-arches on the tone, singing "one, one, one, one."
2. On the fifth "one," gear in your mind the interval of a second, which will release the energy to cover this interval. Sing "two." The rebound will create a flight, sending the hand-arch immediately to the original position of "one." Pulse and sing "one."
3. Continue springing intervals for the entire octave, watching the energy output in relation to the interval size.
4. Add the half-step, which feels ingrown. It uses only half the energy of a whole step.

Could we compare the margin of nature with its over-curve turning direction for the climax with the once further extension of the climax of a phrase or harmonic beat?

Experiencing melodic intervals on the keyboard
1. Gear in your mind an energy charge necessary for a specific interval. This gearing is the moment in which the energy is mobilized to cover the interval experience whole. Your body relates to materialize it.
2. Experience a finger-drop resting down into the keybed, simultaneously realizing the energy charge for an interval of a 5th.
3. Notice the resistance of the keybed to this finger pressure which turns the direction of the energy creating the flight of the rebound covering the interval span. The rebound should lift the arch to its limits with a backward thrust which carries the hand-arch over to cover the second note outlining the interval. On this note's climax reverse the energy's flight to return to 1.
4. Next repeat the above action cycle for each of the other various intervals for 1 to 8, always being aware of the "once further" pressure into the keybed which creates the rebound to cover the interval.

Exercise for harmonic interval-lock position
1. Put your hand down on the keys with the fingers spread out.
2. Gear in your mind a particular interval.
3. Lift the back-arch up to its maximum peak, drawing the fingers up into a rounded finger position, holding down only the fingers outlining the interval.
4. Now rest the back hand-arch over onto the anterior arch, keeping both arches firmly sprung.
5. As you rest down you can feel the interval locked into the hand-arch so that it could be repeated anywhere on the piano you chose to play. Remember: you come to the top of the lock every time you play the interval.

Locking the arch is a great help in playing rapid intervals smoothly and effortlessly. The interval size, locked in the arch, is ready to be played any time, anywhere on the piano.

Consecutive harmonic intervals, 3rds, 4ths and octaves

    1. In ascending with the right hand for 3rds, 4ths and octaves, hold down the 5th finger as the arch rebounds over it covering the next harmonic series.

       Descending with the right hand, hold the thumb down as the rebound carries over it for the next hand-arch position.

    2. In the left hand the alternate fingers will be used. This careful application of the rebound over the sustained note insures a legato quality even though only one of the two fingers is connecting the interval.

    3. An immediate rebound covering the next arch position is essential if a smooth octave passage is attained.

       The more rapid the passage the more immediate the rebound. A moment is reached in which it feels and sounds as if the motion of the whole absorbs the physical adjustments into one experience of smooth on-going.

Creative Motion Highlights

    Our bodies must be fluid enough to match the demands of the Space Age.

    Intervals always rest on the flight created by the rebound.

    Train the ear to hear on the first note of the interval its eventual size. You hear the energy release with its finger-drop not as tone but as power designated for its particular purpose of covering space.

    The joy is in hearing the things which you have sensed.

HARMONIC BEATS

One of the most helpful contributions which Creative Motion has given to the understanding of music is the study of *Harmonic Beat.* Harmony, with its many stages of gradual growth, has been accepted as an element in the music of the western world for almost four centuries. Even a lay opinion about music would pivot around the idea that when two or more tones are sounded together a new "something" is born. Accoustical specialists can count the rate of vibrations that blend or do not blend when united; the overtones of a monochord intimate the triad. But all of these, interesting as they are, try to give evidence of the fact of harmony, to explain what harmony is, not what harmony does. If music is the sound of motion, it is the doing that is important. In the doing its power and its purpose are made clear.

A harmonic beat is the throb that lies within the harmony. It comes where the harmony articulates. It is the feeling center of aliveness in music, a pulse felt intuitively so that once a song is played a throng of people will undulate unconsciously to its inevitable beat.

Whatever the harmonic beat does, it starts at the center. A creative force always starts at the center where the influencing threads of power converge. So we will watch for its motion on the inside always. Interestingly enough, the center of aliveness of the harmonic beat coincides with the center of aliveness of our bodies: the diaphragm, for it is the diaphragm that responds with accurate immediacy to the harmonic beat pulse of music. Rhythm, with its note-value timing, throws quickly to the edges. It is the action loop that thrives on the objective definition. But harmonic beat motion reveals itself in the feeling loop where color and content emerge slowly. It is an unfolding through its entire length and becomes the basic structure out of which the melody naturally flows.

A harmonic beat is made on a throb at the diaphragm with a body follow-through or expansion that comes "over the top," climaxes and returns to center on its release. The "once further" is energy extension. This furthest extension makes possible the change of direction, the complete release and the return of the remaining energy flight. The climax is always the "turn-over" of the motion at the end of the "ah" breath and the extension.

Harmonic beat motion is ever-creative. The force of the impulse spans to the climax, the force of the climax spans to the new impulse. However the climax will never be experienced either in the body or the music unless one extends his whole self to the "once further" with its directional turn-over and release. It is comparable to the stretching of the mighty waters of a wave just as the white-cap turns its force to release itself into the eddying trough below. Like the furthest extension of the wave before the white-cap, so the "once further" with its directional turn onto the climax assures the continued life of the harmonic beat.

Creativity always begins with the *Feeling* loop, then throws to the *Action* loop for its definition.

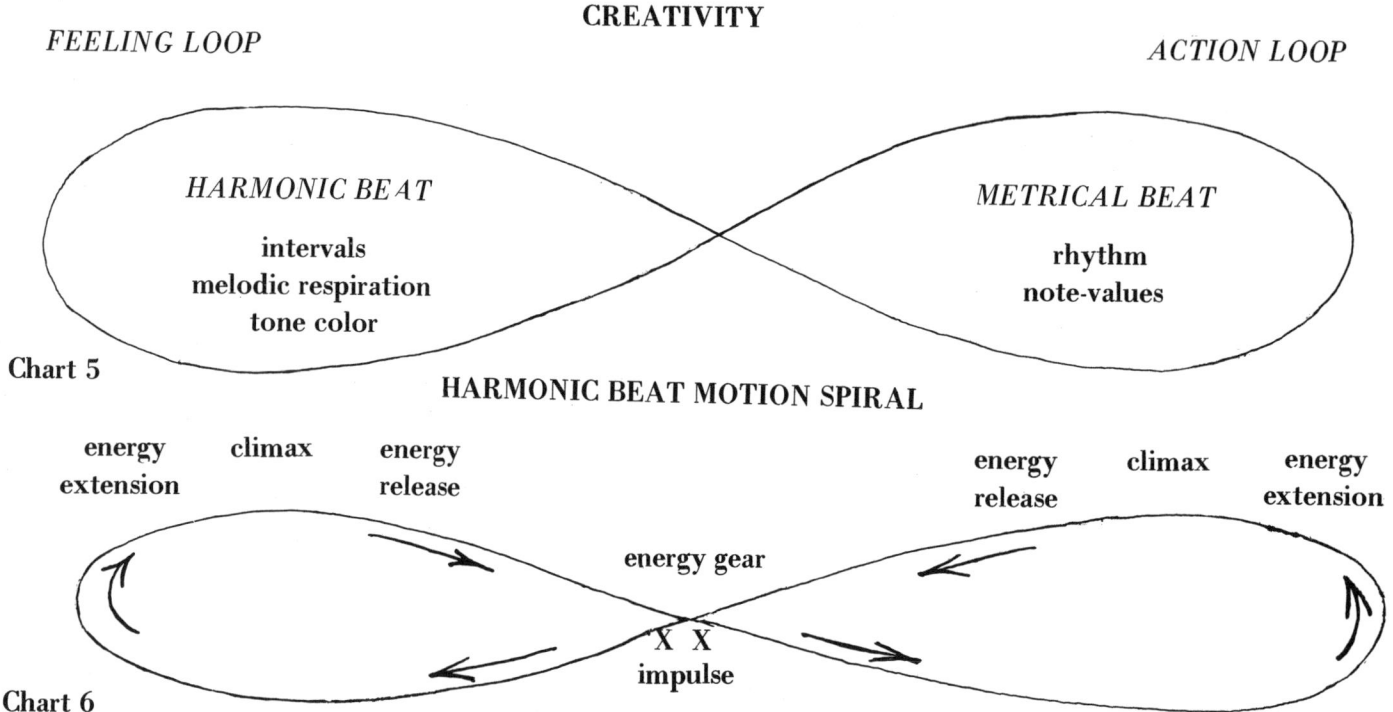

Chart 5

Chart 6

In a spiral the spring at the center of the motion causes the two loops to work in relation to each other.

The history of the harmonic beat would almost be considered the history of homophonic and harmonic music. This, of course, does not imply that harmony and the harmonic beat are one and the same thing. Up to a certain point they are "one and the same" — simultaneous tones united, and in that union a new auditory sensation is born known as a chord: a oneness of tonal experience.

But let us go a step further and view harmony and harmonic beat by way of another comparison, that of relationships. We have said before, "Nothing has value without relationship." What about these tones united together? What gives them meaning? How can we estimate their full value? If we look, we see three notes, written one above the other. We would hear them as a tonal unit, a chord. But heard alone it lacks the relationship to give it prime value. In adding one more chord we increase its meaning, we make firm our evaluation. We now hear the G as the root of the chord, the F-sharp going to G assures the G's position as the root of the chord, the center of the tonal complex. The relationship is that of the dynamic pull of tones toward a center of equilibrium. The relationship could be that of the tones pulling away from the center if the creative desire is one of further expanse of tonal motion, dissonance, adventure, a going away that there might be a return.

Both harmony and harmonic beats are alike in these two qualities — oneness and dynamic relationships. But harmonic beats go beyond these similarities. A harmonic beat is the pulse within, the throb of energy which holds the whole drama of the energy pattern. It is this that makes the harmonic beat unique, the motion of energy made perceptible.

This energy pulse is not altogether dependent upon a chordal texture to give it life. We find the same pulse in monophonic and polyphonic music, where independent lines of melody moving forward with their ceaseless flow have a throb of energy at the center of each tone. This explains the reason why a melodic line, interspersed in the lower voice, can be the expression of a harmonic beat on each note forming this bass melody, a vestige of the polyphonic texture.

In music we experience the passing of time in its most crystalline form and so you might argue: "Time sends the tones on with a throb". But energy is set apart from the necessities of *Time*. Energy knows no limitations or disciplines of time. Energy was at the center of the earth when life began.

To continue our search one step further, the harmonic beat is heard as an interplay of both the polyphonic and homophonic textures. The textures merge, but the harmonic beat is always there. Gradually the chordal aspect of music (so dear to the heart of Bach in his chorales), felt tight and heavy to the classical and romantic composers. They took the chord, stretched it out, changed its position and purpose, like fishermen stretching their nets on the sands to dry. The nets still remain, only their shape and position are changed. So in music when the harmonic beat is taken away from its chordal identity, expressing its one energy throb, and the notes of the chord are opened in sequence, the one throb (on the lowest note of the sequence) still remains. Out of this one pulse the many tones stretched out in time find their way along the path of the harmonic beat's energy charge.

In starting to study a composition we suggest that you read and work on the harmonic beat structure first, for it is the basic structure. The lower note of the harmonic beat is the one that gives the harmonic beat its initial spark. It is the core of the beat to which the other tones bear allegiance. These lower tones of the harmonic beat, when played, form a melodic design.

Since we believe that it is through the body medium that we learn the inner workings of music, let us look at this chart of the harmonic balances.

Harmonic Balances

1. Every harmonic beat registers at the diaphragm, with the head arch balanced over it.

2. The balance of the harmonic beat is the diaphragm over the arm, a structural relationship that frames and establishes the beat.

3. The balances in the arm are determined by the time-space between one harmonic beat and the next harmonic beat.

4. The segment of the arm must be perfectly strong, but rested on the hand arch.

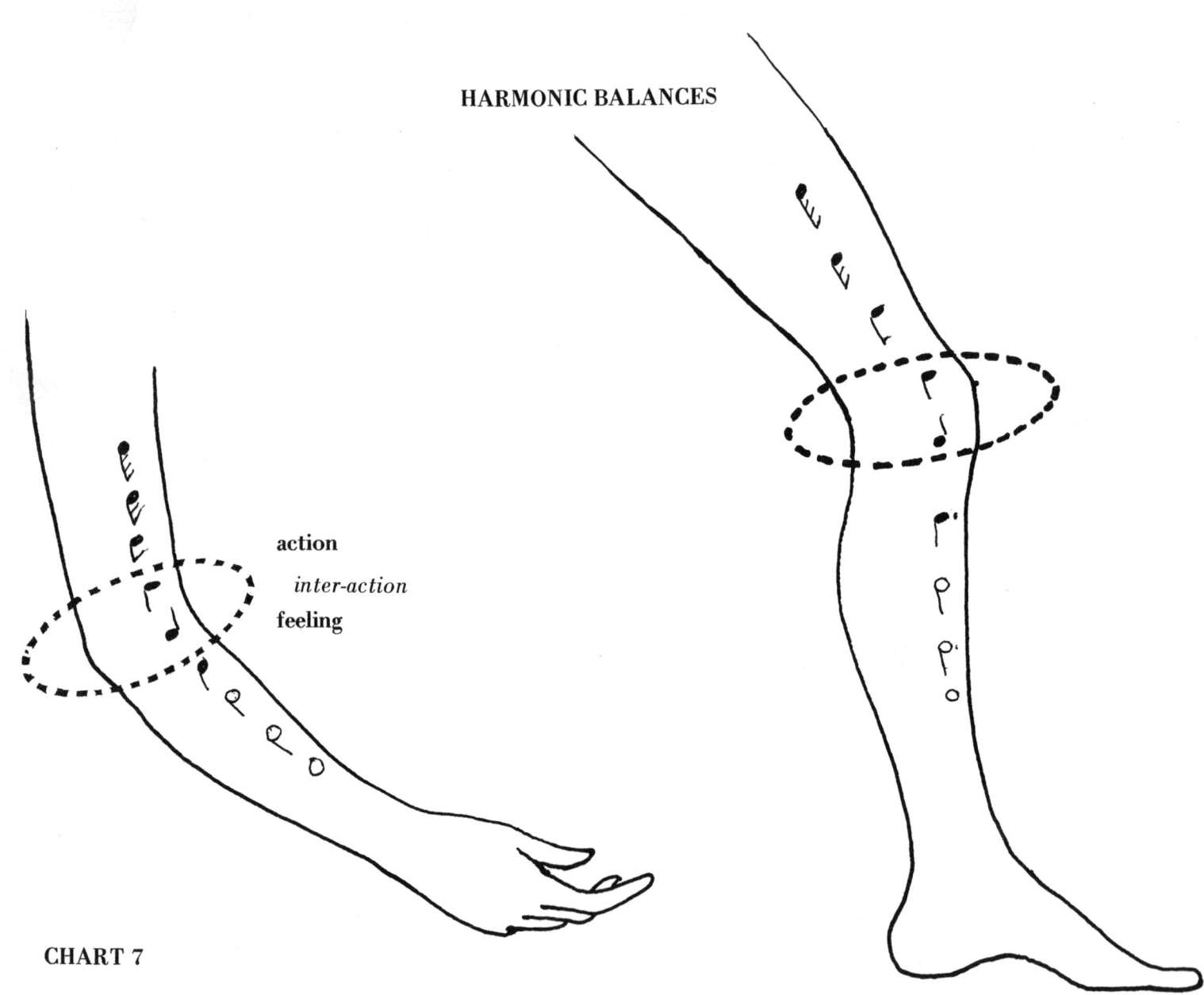

CHART 7

Just as the feeling loop in Chart 5 throws its creative power to the action loop, and the action loop frees its definition in order to make possible a new feeling impulse, hence the harmonic balances direct their power to the melodic balances in order that the creative force can find its tonal definition in the hand-arch and fingers.

If we study these harmonic and melodic balances still closer, we will find that the elbow serves as the breathing center of the harmonic balances, the hand-arch as the breathing center for the melodic balances. These are the two places where the energy extension of the harmonic beat turns over creating the climax, the moment in which inhalation releases to exhalation.

Each level of balances has a pivotal reaction on the other. A half-note balance in the arm automatically comes to rest on the half-note balance point in the hand-arch. And see what happens when you change your balance for sixteenth notes. Without any planned effort on your part the natural liaison between the harmonic and melodic levels insures a forward arch and fine-edged fingertip definition.

You have two things to do in reading harmonic beats:
1. Cover for the intervals, which includes gearing the energy charge in relation to the interval size.
2. Fill the space from harmonic beat to harmonic beat with content.

For the first requirement we take the interval training which we previously outlined in our section on intervals and apply it to harmonic beats. This means not only to name the interval size before you play: "up a fourth, down a fifth," etc., but to gear your energy charge to fit the interval needs in order to cover that much space.

There is always an energy explosion on every harmonic beat, with each explosion having a different rate of force according to its musical content. "Cover" is the body "follow through" of this energy charge. It is instantaneous at the moment the beat starts. The energy is released immediately and throws to the edges (arches of hands, feet and head).

"Content" depends upon the body response to the energy motion. To fill the space with content sounds difficult to do, but not if you remember the journey of the yawn: the "timing" and "touch"* that releases the energy charge, the going on and out with the body extension resulting in the "over-the-top" climax, its change of direction and the final energy release with its return to center, ready for a new impulse. When you fill in with content, it is the body following this energy pattern. In playing the piano it is the readiness, the finger drop with its "once further" creating the rebound, the extension before the climax, the release and the return. It is the structured journey of Creative Motion.

"But what about the right hand?" a pupil may ask. "After all, we can't leave that out, can we?"

"No indeed. The melody tones on the harmonic beats are just as important a part of the structure as the lower notes, but in a different way."

The harmonic beat with its inner feeling pulse, plus the melody with its outside edge, are the two evidences of harmonic form. This feeling or intuitive beat springs the melody. They are co-creative.

---

* See Harmonic Beat Organization #4 and #5; page 78.

Each harmonic beat contains three qualities:
1. length — the quality of "cover": the body extension from one harmonic beat to the next.
2. breadth — the quality of initial spring,
3. color — the feeling quality of the chord structure with its natural body response.

The motion of the top tones of the harmonic beats we term the *Melodic Respiration* (a melody that breathes with tonal life). It is the coordinator of inner feeling and outer expression. It is the melodic shape dependent upon the energy thrust of the harmonic beat. We listen and feel its motion as it moves up and down, molded by an inner force. If the note is lateral (going up in pitch), you extend laterally with an energy inhalation. If the melody tones go down, you feel the vertical line with its energy exhalation and release.

We are really watching the direction of the melodic intervals on the harmonic beats, the lateral and vertical lines as they respond to each other. If the melodic tones are thrust higher and higher in pitch, you become more and more lateral with a wider and wider feeling filling all of the space around you. (It is an irresistible idea to relate the intensity of vibration the higher in pitch one goes to the intensity of feeling one gets by lateral increase.) If the melodic respiration turns its direction, your body, including your foot arches, feels a "banking" to compensate for the directional shift, and your balance now becomes vertical. The first melodic respiration note on the first harmonic beat of a composition, or section thereof, is always lateral. This is universally true. The following brief outline may help.

Lateral: wide line, hand-arch focus, rest on 5th finger, inhalation.
Vertical: tall line, head and foot-arch focus, rest on thumbs, exhalation.

It is a prevalent tendency for pianists, professional or otherwise, to be right-handed players. This is partly because man is a right-handed creature by birth and learned skills, and partly because the outside edge of form (melody) is more easily heard than the inner voices. But with music this right-handed aptitude weakens the effect of the natural power created in the music. As you know, creativity, including re-creation, starts on the inside, sparked by feeling. Harmonic beat, as evidenced by the feeling loop coupled with its melodic respiration tone, is a left to right-handed process. If this approach is part of the learning it will cure the over-indulgence of the right-handed tendency. We must synchronize our hands. If we realize that their strength, simultaneously given, comes from one central source, the diaphragm; if we learn through experience that the right hand rides on the power of the left; and if we know that our arms and hands are "one pair" rather than two separate members, our hands *will* become synchronized and our music will have, therefore, a new unity and tonal significance. Remember: it is only through the diaphragm that this synchronization can take place.

"But what happens to the other melody notes not on a harmonic beat? What do they do?" you ask.

The other melody notes not on a harmonic beat are played off of the anterior (front) arch with clear finger articulation on the flight from one harmonic beat to another. In every flight there is an arc of motion. On the harmonic beat the hand-arch takes the arc moving through it until the next harmonic beat. All of the tones between the harmonic beats ride the motion of the arc being played off of the front arch. It sounds and feels as if the notes were being "poured out" rather than "played out". If there are no notes other than the harmonic beats, the back hand-arch does not settle over on the anterior arch until the climax of the harmonic beat. This adjustment of balance in the arch gives a "ping" to the tone when rightly made. It also makes possible better timing and touch for the next harmonic beat.

The harmonic color is the feeling that the harmony arouses in the listener. The harmonic beat throws the chordal balances; you experience them with your body. You hang over the top of the feeling as you hear the color quality of the next chord to which your body responds. You never leave the color experience of the harmonic beat. Harmonic color is born out of the relationship of tone to tone. In a previous section we talked of the dynamic power of tones, that which gives them their musical meaning, that which allows each tone its particular place in the tonal expanse. This being true of single tones, how much more intense is the feeling when three tones, rather than one, are taking their place in the dynamic field of force.

"And what of the body relation to harmonic color? What does it do?"

The body *becomes* the "feeling," it is the prototype of the harmonic color. Certainly sculpture from the earliest days of Greek art to the present proves to us that the body holds the key to feeling. Certainly the three basic triads should be anticipated and honored with a body balance response.

- I   Tonic covers center — "I am"
- IV Subdominant covers back of center — "I would"
- V   Dominant covers forward — "I will".

Included are the building chord structures with their natural physical response evoked from the tension or equilibrium of the tones. However, they only suggest to you that which you must find out for yourself by hearing, feeling and doing.

- I   Lateral and vertical in equilibrium. The body feels balanced on all arches freely.
- II   Dissonance, pulled inside of self, self-pitying, begrudging.
- III Minor of V, so has action but subdued.
- IV   Balanced back of center, hopeful, asking, "amen" cadence.
- V   Balanced forward on front foot, feeling of action at eye level.
- VI   Minor of I. Resigned with a lowered diaphragm, poised and serene.
- VII Eager for arrival, forward moving, attained by slightly lowering the diaphragm.

HARMONIC BEAT ORGANIZATION

The Pulse: is the tiny throb at the center of the diaphragm, impelled by the music.

Melodic Respiration: is the melodic shape created by the energy thrust of each harmonic beat. There is an adjustment of the outer line of movement of the body to the inner line of force of the music evoking a lateral (wide), vertical (tall) response. The response of the hands, feet and head are identical with the body movement.

Harmonic Color: is the feeling quality of the chord structure effected by tonal dynamics, with its natural body response.

Timing: is the energy charge of the harmonic beat, the initial motion of the energy release. It is determined by the faster note in the harmonic beat complex whether in the right hand or left. The energy release is two stranded. The TIMING strand must reach its climax at half of the value of the faster note and is there suspended until the other strand, uniting with the body weight balances, moves along with the movement of the song. The two strands unite at the climax of the harmonic beat.

Touch: is the impact with the key. The touch releases the energy flight of the harmonic beat. It is the same for both hands making up the harmonic beat.

Cover: is the action end or body "follow through" of TIMING. You spring the cover as you rest down to play the initial note of the harmonic beat. While the finger tips go further and further into the keys, the arch rebounds to cover the next harmonic beat, as the hand-arch follows the arc of motion created by the flight of the harmonic beat. The hand-arch and fingers should be poised over the next harmonic beat at the climax of the beat now being held. The arch and fingers stay as high as the flight springs them until they drop down to play. Any melody that comes as an aftermath of the harmonic beat throb, but is dependent upon it, is molded on the front (anterior) arch.

The Rebound: is created by the oppositional force of the finger-drop pressure to the resistance of the key bed. The rebound is redirecting this force which, in turn, creates the flight.

The Flight: is a two stranded flight of energy. The "feeling" strand goes at once to the climax and waits there suspended while the "action" strand, directing the body motion, moves along with the time-space evaluation of the music. Both strands unite at the climax of the harmonic beat with its final release of the remaining energy.

The Arch: The harmonic beat is held whole in the hand-arch. The notes falling out of the beat but extended in time come off of the front arch. The back hand-arch adjusts its balance to make this arch adjustment possible.

Balances: the harmonic beat balances are the weight balances in the arm, and are determined by the time-space between one harmonic beat and the next one. To keep the tone in the keys, your weight balances move along with the movement of the song.

Metrical Beat: The harmonic beat cannot be without metrical beat which is the time-space of "action," the opposite side of the "feeling" loop. The rhythmic value of the harmonic beat determines the weight balances in the arm, which are inter-related to the melodic balances in the hand-arch and fingers.

The Climax: the action strand of the flight goes immediately to the hand-arch moving along with the motion of the music. After the "once further" which redirects the energy creating the climax, the hand-arch settles over onto the anterior arch making ready for the new harmonic beat. Letting the elbow breathe the motion of the "once further" extension and "turn over" will aid in the feeling of the climax.

Extension: the Body-strand of the energy release following through time and space the pathway of the Time-strand of the energy charge. From impulse to climax it is experienced as an energy inhalation, from the climax to the next impulse it is experienced as an energy exhalation.

ALL THROUGH THE NIGHT

Welsh · Traditional English words

Harmonic Beat Exercises Using "All Through The Night"

1. Stand with the diaphragm balanced over the feet. The feet are in direct relation to the harmonic beat pulse. Have a tuned light-weight-body as you listen to "All Through the Night."
2. Match the music by thinking and feeling a spring at the center of the diaphragm. Rest all of yourself on the experience. Hear-feel the place where the harmonic beat "goes over the top" ready for the change of direction and return. The climax comes just at the "turn-over" which makes possible the release of energy and its return. This you do with your body as the music plays.
3. Place your hands crossed at the diaphragm as you continue pulsing with the music. Rest on the first harmonic beat covering the next one. Hear-feel the harmonic beat pulse in the hand arches. Since the diaphragm is a sheath of muscle, the harmonic beat spiral can rotate in any directional combination. It is best to start at the center and spring back and up for the first loop, compensated by a forward spring to complete the spiral.
4. Now extend your arms out at the side. Feel as if they rested down on the air. Let the arms swing from the diaphragm as you follow the folk song's harmonic beat structure. Watch your arms follow the inner pulse of the diaphragm with absolutely no muscular motion of their own. Remember that it is the energy extension and change of direction that makes possible another harmonic beat.
5. Now put your attention onto the melodic respiration. Feel your body shift its balance in response to the lateral-vertical motion of the melody. It is a subtle inside motion, like the closing and opening breath of a butterfly's wings. When you rest on a harmonic beat, the energy registers either a "wide" or a "tall."

More Harmonic Beat Exercises Using "All Through The Night"

1. Now go to the keyboard. Sit with the diaphragm balanced over the foot arches. The harmonic beat pulse extends to the feet always. This relation is important for the use of the pedal. The head arch also must be balanced over the diaphragm. Reaffirm your light-weight-body.
2. Rest your hands on the piano ledge with your diaphragm rested over them. The motion of the music will start the inner pulse of the beat. Feel the force of the harmonic beat swing over the hand-arch as it combines with the swing at the diaphragm. Match the motion on the inside always; never let the outside fix up the inside. Feel your body fill all of the space until it is ready to rest on the next harmonic beat. The hands respond to this arc of motion.
3. Now put your attention on the melodic respiration of the folksong, letting your hands, still

on the piano ledge, follow the lateral-vertical motion as the music suggests. Lateral with its widening inhalation or vertical with its exhalation and release of power. The breathing suggested here is an energy breath not a lung breath, although sometimes they flow together in an effortless manner.

4. As you play the harmonic beats, sing the melodic respiration, saying "lateral going to vertical going to lateral", etc. Feel the banking in your hand-arches as you change direction on the climax of the note (half of its metrical value). You play a lateral note with a lateral line in both your body and hand. At the climax of this tone you cover a vertical melody note in your body and hand-arch ready for its finger-drop.

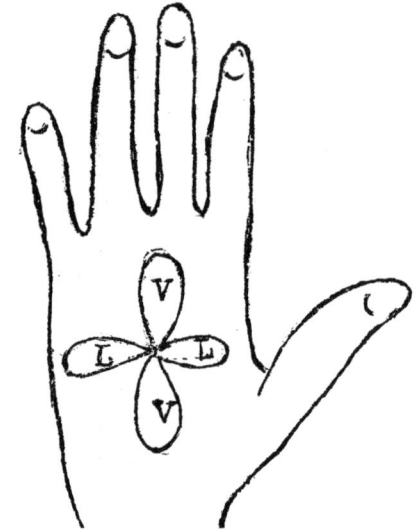

Rest all of yourself on the hand arches.

The "feeling strand" of energy goes immediately to the next wide or tall, the "action" strand fills in with the body.

Watch the body fill in all of the space until it is ready to rest on the next harmonic beat melody note, either lateral or vertical.

At the climax of the harmonic beat the arch has arrived at a position ready to play the next harmonic beat with a shift in melodic respiration if the music demands it.

MELODIC RESPIRATION ARCH
Chart 8

5. To help further your melodic sensitivity, play a section of a composition that you are studying. As you play put your attention on the melodic respiration motion. Feel the rise and fall of the melodic intervals with their accompanying body response and hand banking. Hear the subtle shading of tone as a result of the body "follow through," not only in response to the melodic line but to the note-value timing. If the body honestly yields to the quiet shifts of motion balance as the melodic intervals dictate, it increases the chance that the melody notes, as tonal off-shoots of the harmonic beat, will not intrude themselves as they so frequently do, but will take their place as an anterior arch floral design between the pillars of the harmonic beat framework.

6. In playing a harmonic beat the hand-arch rises to its maximum as a rebound from the oppositional force created by the resting down finger pressure against the key bed. As the harmonic beat note is being held, the hand arch molds the going up and over the arc of motion in order to cover the next harmonic beat at the climax of the note now being held. At this climax the energy which has been pouring through the finger as it presses further into the key bed is released to cover the next harmonic beat. The weight of the arm balance is always transferring from "where it is to where it is going."

"Does the arch rebound only on the harmonic beats or also on the intermediary notes on the way to the next harmonic beat?" The finger drop gets a rebound kick against the arch for every note it plays.

"Is the energy charge which sends out the melody the same as the energy charge for the interval?" Yes, the charge that sends out the interval (harmonic, "feeling") is the same as that sent out for the melodic shape ("action").

7. Since the foot-arch is always in response to the diaphragm, and the harmonic beat depends

upon the tiny throb at the diaphragm's center for its very existence, we realize the necessity of relating the use of the pedal to the study of harmonic beats. The back foot is the "feeling" foot, so keep it back. It helps to give a sustained balance to the front or "action" foot. The oppositional force created by the pressure of the back foot against the floor and that of the pelvis against the piano bench throws the motion of the music. The pedal is the foot-arch way of bracing the harmonic beat pulse, besides enriching and amplifying the harmonic beat's tonal motion. The soft pedal has no influence on the harmonic beat pulse. It only subdues the tone, therefore when the soft pedal is no longer needed, the left foot should return to its place of body support. In general, polyphonic music needs no pedal. In this musical texture every bass note is a harmonic beat along with its accompanying melody note. Only in rare moments, when the harmonic texture asserts itself, can the pedal be used and then only sparingly.

The arch spring in the foot comes simultaneously with the finger-drop. The spring lifts the front part of the foot up (as the fingers rest down into the keys), then goes down immediately. The faster the note values, the farther forward your pedal leverage becomes.

The diaphragmatic pulse on each harmonic beat extends to both the "feeling" foot-arch and the "action" foot-arch by way of radiant coordination. Feel the "coming up" sensation in the spring of the foot arch.

8. When a rest follows a note in a harmonic beat structure, the rest is always contained in the note. The harmonic beat takes both note and rest. The rest is added to the time-space value of the harmonic beat. If a rest has taken the place of a note in the melody over a harmonic beat and is the faster of the two notations, the rest will determine the timing of the energy charge.

When harmonic beats are opened up and extended in time, as in waltz rhythm, arpeggios, Alberti bass, sonatina, barcarole, lullaby, the general rule of one pedal for each harmonic beat is observed. But always your ear must give the final verdict.

There are three basic harmonic beat structural possibilities:

1. If the structure is chordal, then each chord is a harmonic beat even if the chord is repeated. Example – Chopin's C minor Prelude, page 123.

2. If the bass notes form a melodic line, then each bass melody note is a harmonic beat, each one of equal importance.

A variation of this same structure is given in the examples below:

Here the harmonic beats are on the lower quaver of each beat, since they form the bass melody pattern.

In the example above, the notes forming the bass melody are not the lowest notes of the quarter note series.

3. If certain bass notes qualify as the lower note of an open chord structure, then just the lowest note of each harmonic grouping is a harmonic beat, the other notes issue out of it, unfolding in "time".

Examples of Harmonic Beat Structures

The rhythmic structure of a march basically responds to the bi-lateral motion of marching feet. There are two harmonic beats to a measure, on the first and third counts. This structure is sometimes necessarily altered for cadences as in the second measure of example A.

A waltz throws the energy charge of the harmonic beat from the first beat to the first beat of each measure. Since a waltz is in 3/4 time, the climax of each harmonic beat comes between the second and the third beats. This means that the climactic extension with its "over the top" lift is experienced without metrical definition. This is the very quality that puts life and a subtle flowing grace into a waltz. Without this conscious experience a waltz goes dead.

84

The lowest note of the arpeggio releases the harmonic beat for its entire curve of motion. The top note is not another harmonic beat nor an accented tone, but it is the climax of the harmonic beat out of which the descent is released. In the following example (Chopin Etude op 25 No. 12) the first note of the third beat must not be delivered nor felt as a second harmonic beat, but it must be the climactic fulfillment of the harmonic beat extension.

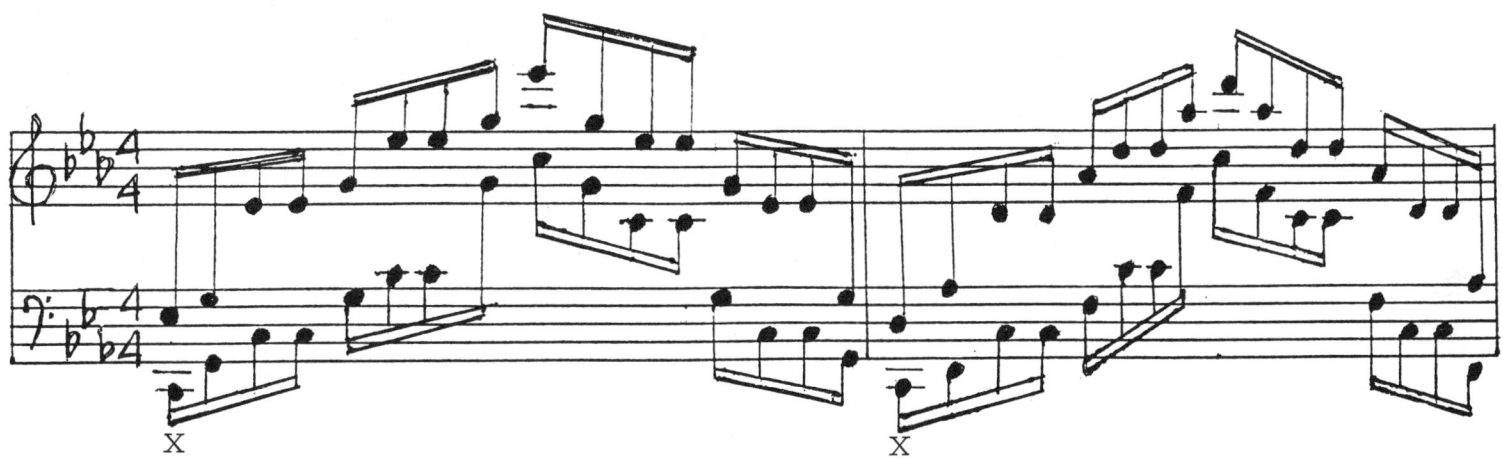

The 6/8 rhythm of a barcarole is excellent training for feeling the difference between 6/8 and 3/4 timing. With only one harmonic beat to the measure there will be less tendency to allow the 4th beat the impact of a 1st beat. Instead, the fourth beat as the harmonic beat climax will necessarily be felt on the top of the curve of motion. If the motion is felt on the inside, one pedal for each harmonic beat will be sufficient and correct unless the idiom changes.

The lullabye also has one harmonic beat to a measure with a gentle melody flowing out of it. The lower note of the harmonic beat usually stays on the same pitch. The cradle rocks, but it does not change its position on the floor. One hears a lullabye as quiet motion because of this reiteration.

HARMONIC BEAT BALLOON PLAY

Tossing balloons with a gentle arch thrust, timed to the flow of music with "follow through" of the hand arch, arm, and body, becomes the extraverted experience of harmonic beat. It is not only to watch the balloon's pathway of released energy, marked by its rise and fall, but to evaluate the necessary energy thrust in relation to the desired musical journey of the balloon.

The gearing must involve the right amount of energy for the gentle lifting up of the small space craft experience. It is not a "hit" with the action hand arch, rather it is the involvement of the harmonic part of the arm with its "follow through" that makes it a timed and beautiful motion.

To time the flight so that the climax is reached in the balloon ascent to match the climax of the music is the perfection sought in the motion. If these climactic moments are identical in time, the return for the new impulse of motion will also be synchronized with the music.

Besides this particular learning, balloons train the ear to be aware of the lower harmonic beat voice — a double duty for the ear which turns listening from the usual melodic approach to listening "in depth."

THE METRIC WAVE

Phrase form starts with harmonic beat motion. Harmonic beat cannot function without metrical beat, the time-space of action. Since we have not included metre in our study except indirectly, let us now look at metre and see how it fits into Creative Motion.

"Metre divides the flow of time into equal time units" is the definition most widely accepted. From this definition we can easily make a graph to chart the course of metre.

|⎯⎯⎯⎯|⎯⎯⎯⎯|⎯⎯⎯⎯|⎯⎯⎯⎯|⎯⎯⎯⎯|⎯⎯⎯⎯|⎯⎯⎯⎯|⎯⎯⎯⎯|⎯⎯⎯⎯|⎯⎯⎯⎯|⎯⎯⎯⎯|⎯⎯⎯⎯|⎯⎯⎯⎯|

Here it is: Time shown as the unending line, marked off into equal time units. We are given the choice of counting either a continuous 1-1-1, or a numerical continuum ad infinitum. There we can leave the definition and graph.

But looking back with experiential perspective there is surely something wrong. It may be a graph of metre, but it is not a metric graph of music. The numbers indicate clearly enough that our graph is not illustrating musical time, for who would ever count from 1 to 3,698 for a Beethoven sonata, or where is the conductor who does not look beyond the beat of 1?

Let us forget the "even time units" and start with the other part of the definition: "It divides the flow of time." "Flow." Flowing means motion, and nothing moves without energy. So here we have Time and Motion! With "time" we are face to face with the one thing which man knows has no beginning or ending, a formless unending round of going-onness. Only man's experience with time, his life pattern, has shape and form. It is here that music helps to interpret time, not as something formless, but as something having unending design and pattern.

The measurement of energy into "equal time units" must be as eternal as time itself. What then would the graph be? Or could it be symbolized?

After groping for answers we are back at our spiral, the sign of infinity in science. The released energy of the impulse thrust throws to the climax; the climax flows to the new impulse on the remaining release of energy. The balance of the forces will keep this motion going on forever.

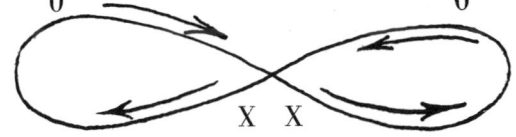

The going away and return of the Metric Wave

Our spiral indicates by its crossing of lines that there must be a return in the motion. There is always a going away in every return. How else could it be? You cannot come back unless you are "not there" at some moment in time. This is the place where the wave and musical metre join hands. The wave is the physical evidence which energy has made for music with its energy release, its "over-the-top" climax, and its return for another "going away." Putting the numbers into the design is self-evident. The "going away" of 1 must have in it the power to return to 1. The metric wave is the eternal life of metre, and perhaps the eternal measurement of the life-flow of time, for nature is built on the *Law of Return*. It is the inner spirit of Life made manifest.

The great challenge for us as musicians is that we can use this metric wave concept to such precious purpose. Whenever we are concerned with metre, which is always, for it is the "action" loop of the creative spiral, we should be concerned with its form and its flow. So now metre, with the usual counting aloud *1 2 3 4* all on a straight line; the metronome, industrious as it is; or beating one's foot on the floor, should all be rejudged by our knowledge of the metric wave.

Counting for a metric wave could never sound as if all of the numbers were on a straight line, since the counting is verbalizing an arc of motion. The metronome gives no inkling of a "going away" and a "return." Beating one's foot on the floor might not be so bad if the motion were centered at the diaphragm, but it usually sounds foot-centered. Yet each one of these procedures is a common practise tool, emphasizing only the outside of metre with total exclusion of its inner motion and meaning.

Because the wave unfolds in time, each one of the metric units will be different, for each one is on a new phase of the energy flow, a variant place on the spiral. How can 2 be like 1 or 3 in 4/4 metre? Or how can 4 be like 2 or 1 since each has his particular place on the energy flight which cannot be metrically duplicated until the new flight is taken?

A metre of 6/8 is usually the glaring example of non-metric-wave playing. Almost all 6/8 metre turns into 3/4 time in the hands of students as well as highly trained musicians. Their music seldom has that long, beautiful sweep of 6/8 motion, with its "over-the-crest" climax on the 4th beat. The body must be ready to sustain the long 6/8 flight before the playing ever begins, otherwise the wide horizontal line will never be expressed.

A Viennese conductor once said to an American audience, "People in this country do not know how to play a waltz! They never include the place where the boy squeezes the girl!" Of course "that place" is the climax of the measure, but a metrically silent one. It comes as has been said between the second and third beats, the turn-over of the energy extension. The subtly graceful climactic turn comes on the "squeeze" — the high point of the metric wave. To omit the squeeze was a musical tragedy!

Before counting aloud one should first hear-feel the metric wave pulsing on the inside. When this inner motion is established, do not begin to play on an impulse, but start on a climax with its turn-over and energy exhalation covering the next impulse. A good exhalation insures a good inhalation.

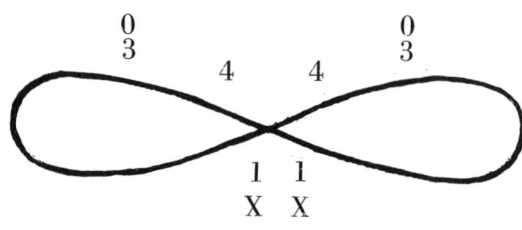

In this chart you see that the count of 2 is not included as an audible numeral, but the space between 1 and 3 indicates that 2 is included as part of the completely whole

Chart 9

motion. We flow past it on an upward arc. Silence on the second count helps to insure the flight covering the climax. If 2 is counted aloud with the same level of voice expression as 1 or 3 (in 4/4 metre) neither the flight nor the wave will ever materialize.

Ride the feeling of the metric wave before the playing begins. It is like inside singing. If it is not there at the center, the periphery can never express the waves' musical worth. When we survey our various approaches to music as the "sound of motion", we realize that the search becomes more and more simple. It is the patterned pathway of energy and our relation to it with our whole selves.

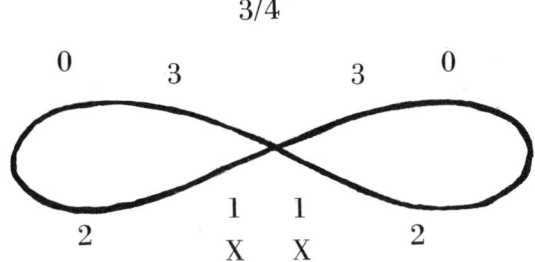

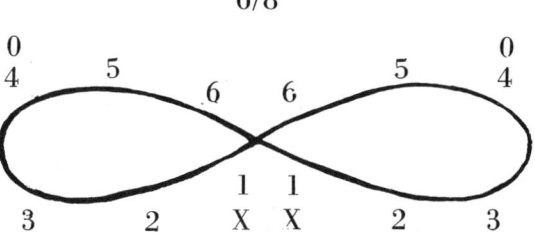

Here the climax comes between the 2nd and 3rd beats. That breathless moment in a waltz.

Chart 10

The "over-the-top" climax in 6/8 metric wave is one of the most fluid and graceful motions in music. Very few pianists achieve it, because they do not feel the metric wave on the inside before they play.

Creative Motion Highlights

Growth is the continued expansion of the individual's musicianship.
Creative Motion teaches us to play from an inner necessity.
To express on the outside, you must rest first on the inside.
We muss up our lives and our music because we attend to the Multiple instead of attending to the focus that makes the Multiplicity ONE.

PHRASE FORM

The musical structures we have been studying have been those of a musical unit: a tone, a metric wave, a note value, a harmonic beat. Each one of these has been a whole within itself, having the same organization found in all living creatures or action processes. It is the life cycle: a beginning, a going on to a high point of action, and a return anticipating a new beginning. In musical terms it consists of an impulse, a climax and a cadence. Each individual unit mentioned above possesses these creative elements, making a whole out of the parts. Now we go one step further and ask: Can these units, grouped together, make a larger and more encompassing whole? We know the answer, for in all life we see levels of development ranging from the smallest unit to the largest depending upon the relationship of the parts within the whole.

In music the responsibility of this union is given to the phrase. *Phrase* is the organizational element in music that gives to music its basic form. The content of the phrase depends completely upon the relationship of the parts from which the whole is created. As the units become interrelated, making up the content of the whole, we find that the creative pattern has not changed; only the bowl into which the phrase content has been poured has become larger and more abundant in size. Phrase, the revealer of the metric wave, the joiner of interval to tone, the emancipator of harmonic beat, the liberator of rhythmic design: phrase uses them all for creating the simplest folk-song or the most majestic musical tapestry of tone.

Let us look at the phrase from the inside and see how it works. Remember, it will not be different in structure from each single unit; it will differ only in degree.

The following diagram is that of *Phrase*:

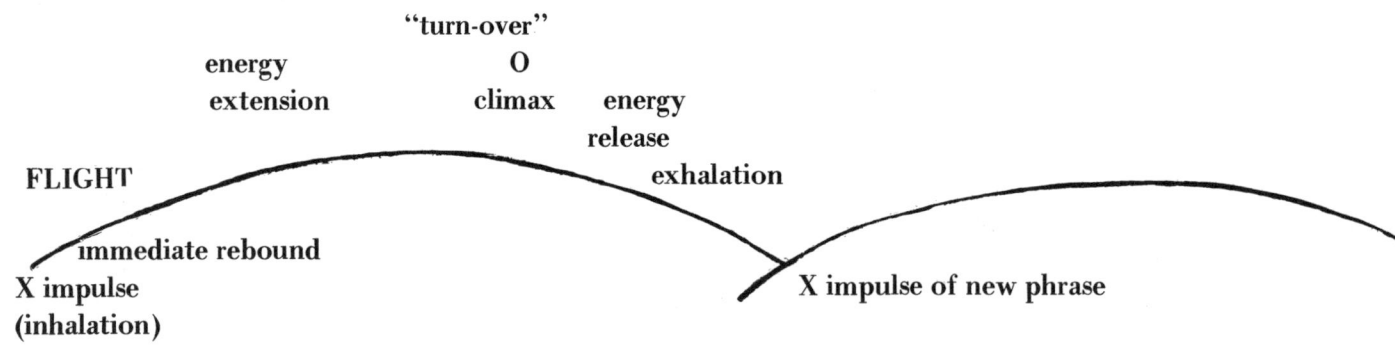

Chart 11

We are learning to mobilize and release our energy for phrase motion in response to a governing idea, with the radiant coordination of the light-weight-body, which insures the parts being related to the whole.

The *Governing Idea* has a choice of action in mind. The energy is flashed whole and mobilized for the complete phrase so that nothing will be left undone. This is *Gearing*, the "get-on-your-mark" sensation, the "ah" breath of the yawn, which takes place in the head arch. This gearing is separated from the release of the energy by only a hair's breadth or the fraction of a millionth part. As this energy charge is held whole within the mind and body (alertness), *Timing* steps in.

Timing is the energy control of the whole output of energy. It is the relation of the inside to the outside, the requisite of power fulfillment. It frees the stored energy for action. Timing puts the body into the frame of the music. A "timed" body is one that contains the necessary energy to compensate for all of the individual needs of the music as well as the need of the whole. It is the spiritual element of activity.

The *Timing* and *Touch* combined release the energy charge on the first note of the phrase preliminary to the *Flight*.

Touch is expressed by the impact with the key and realizes the inside preparation for that particular tone along with the anticipation of the whole. It also realizes the oppositional force of weight and pressure (down) combined with energy (up). This opposition is felt from the fingertips to the top of the head. *Touch* is the *Quality* of the finger-drop, the down-thrust of energy. There must be enough spring in the touch to insure the rebound.

The *Rebound* is created by the "once further" of the finger against the resistance of the key bed; it is the spring-back which produces the *Flight*. The flight becomes a two-stranded expression of energy. First: the "timed" strand goes instantaneously to the climax and hangs there suspended. Second: the action strand uses the body for its medium of motion in order to express the time-space of the music. The two strands join at the climax after the body has filled in with an energy extension which makes the "turn-over" for the climax. The energy release after the climax is immediate. It feels as if the climax pours itself onto the energy exhalation with its final phrase definition. Everything after that is molded on the way to the next impulse with the remaining released energy.

The inner idea equals the outer form and the body is the transfer force from one plane to the other. One must hear or feel or see the form as it unfolds itself in the outer world and know it for the same form one hears or feels or sees inside.

Form is the shape of content. *Content* is the way you use your body to create form. *Creative Motion* is the need to find the inner motion of the music before the outer motion of the music can take place. The body rides the motion of the music regardless of the level at which one concentrates.

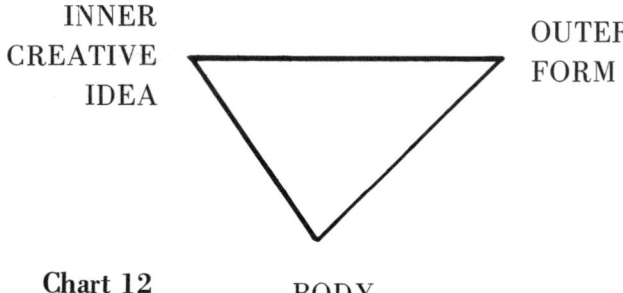

INNER CREATIVE IDEA

OUTER FORM

BODY

Chart 12

With a light-weight-body the will to act springs the energy whole. Without the light-weight-body the oppositional forces are out of balance; the gravitational will supersede the levitational. Because of this lack of balance, the desire will not spring the energy whole.

The head spring (the "ah" of the yawn) then organizes the phrase. Practice to become aware of it in response to the desire to hear the phrase spring whole. This is valid since the climax is actually contained in the impulse. The climax, as you know, is an inevitable result emanating from the energy extension. The "togetherness" of the impulse and climax is comparable to a deep inhalation followed by an "over-the-top" exhalation. It is all the same air, but each breathed in a different direction.

Both the impulse and the climax of the phrase are determined by the energy thrust. The impulse initiates the "feeling" loop, born of previous musical attitudes and experiences. The climax initiates the action or definition loop where the phrase is appraised. After the climax you come back inside of yourself with the feeling of watching the phrase define.

In your final weeks of practice, the governing idea will include the entire composition and flash the energy whole. The whole will encompass all of the parts so that their inter-relation will be made complete. Do not start to play until you know and can realize the definition of the phrase form. Only then will you express the shape and color and content of the music.

Thus phrase is the pattern of energy made incarnate in music.

Feeling The Shape And Quality Of Phrase-Form

The shape of a phrase depends upon the distance between the impulse and the climax, influenced by the energy charge necessary to cover the distance. Metre is the basis by which the distance is measured. The number symbols extend from 1 through 8 irrespective of bars. If the phrase goes beyond 8, continue counting until the climax has been reached, then subtract 8 from that number. This gives the phrase shape plus the added energy extension of the first group of 8.

The quality depends upon the use the music makes of the particular amount of energy charge. Each size will possess its special quality. There is a correlation between the tonal dynamic numbers, the harmonic numerals and the phrase symbols. The feeling content and the body response both verify this numerical principle.

There is an interaction between harmonic beat, metrical beat and phrase (whose impulse and climax is always on a harmonic beat.) The impact of the first beat of a measure is essential to create an impulse of a phrase. Thus phrase is shaped by the inner throb of the harmonic structure plus the extraverted action of metre. A phrase of 3 would be in square metre, a phrase of 4 in round. 6/8 is based on one beat for each ♩, making two beats to a measure. The climax will usually be on a round number.

The Phrase Circle

Stand with the diaphragm balanced over the foot arches. Feel the oppositional forces in equilibrium at the diaphragm. Shoulders rested down.

As you hear-feel the music, release sufficient energy to cover the phrase shape by springing both hands around the imaginative circular form of the phrase you hear. The impulse will be a hand-arch rebound, the extension with its inevitable turn-over will create the climax. The body extension felt as diaphragmatic inhalation will mold the curved motion of the arms.

Exhale completely on the climax with lung breath. Adjust to the phrase shape with your whole body. Practice inside singing for greater sensitivity.

PHRASE OF 1 – The energy release of impulse and climax come together as a sudden burst of aliveness, like birthday candles on a cake all blown out at once.

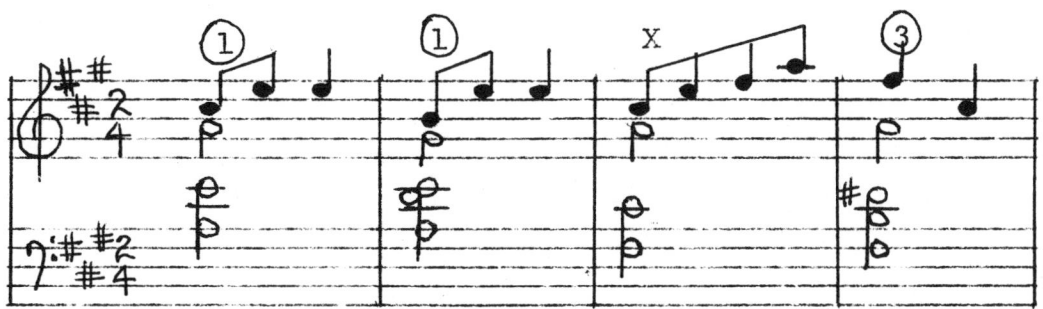

PHRASE OF 2 – Impulse sprung in arch throws the motion to the wrist for the climax. This gives the phrase a dissonant and sharp feeling. It is very edged.

PHRASE OF 3 – This phrase shape is flowing and curved, with the same quality as the tone of 3 in the dynamic field of force.

PHRASE OF 5 – Five has a forward balance with a strong line. Very active. It serves as the "everyday" practical phrase length.

PHRASE OF 4 — Here you stand behind the line as you did on the subdominant chord; or as in tonal dynamics, the natural tendency of 4 to 3.

PHRASE OF 7 — The impact of the arch against the air springs the rebound to a point above the eye-line. The body extension must be very sustained to fulfill this motion.

PHRASE OF 6 — This phrase is irregular. It feels pregnant with weight, which tends to put the balance on the back foot.

PHRASE OF 9 — Subtract 8 from this number and it gives you the color content of the phrase of 1. An immediacy of power which extends over eight counts before the final release at the climax on 9. It is like a sky-rocket whose final star bursts after a long waiting.

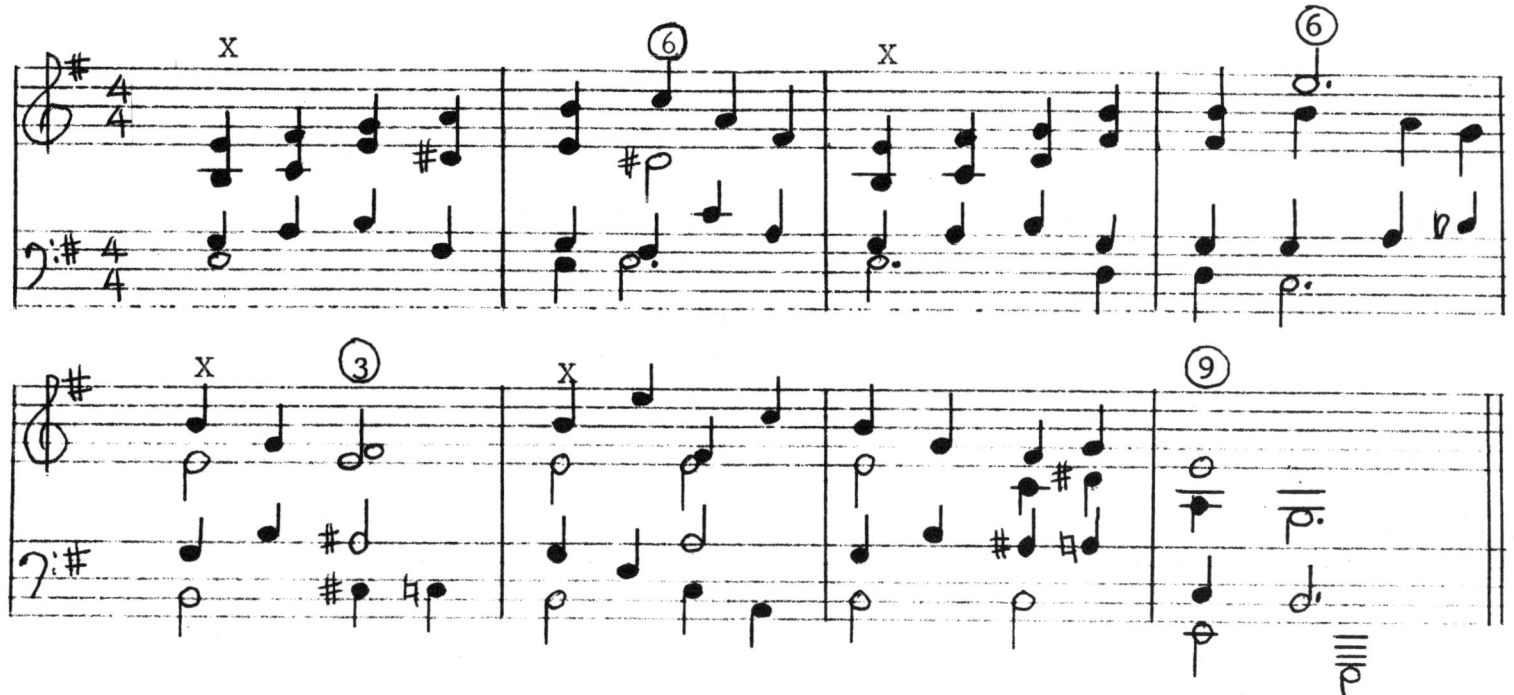

Because Timing relates all of the parts to the whole through its charge of energy, an impulse will cover the following climax; the climax, looking beyond the cadence, will cover the next impulse. You energy-gear for the new phrase (anticipating its shape and quality) on the last harmonic beat of the previous phrase. Thus there will never be a moment in which the music is without the flight of energy. A retard, a pause, a nuance or extended rests must all be felt on the energy curve of the musical motion.

Creative Motion Highlights

You sense the weight balance when you rest down on the impulse. You sense the energy balance on the rebound.
Every whole must have an impulse and a climax. The impluse is the place where the phrase begins to work, the climax is the place where it is realized as the release of form.
Being alive depends upon the fulfillment of breathing.
The body must always be in process toward its fullest extension. This is *Tonicity*.
In the end, after teaching people to listen inside, they must also be able to hear or feel that singing as it sounds outside, or the broadcast of the inner thing one hears will never happen.

OURSELVES IN RELATION TO PHRASE

The *Governing Idea* is your over-all plan for action. Desire causes the *Gearing*. Think the thing you want to do in order to make sure that the energy is mobilized and ready for its release into the world of action.

The "Ah" breath (the yawn feeling) in the head helps to organize the phrase. It alerts you, it chastens you. All of you must be ready for the moment of energy release, for all of the complete motion is contained in the thing to be exploded. Your readiness to "go" sparks the *Timing*, which turns the mobilized energy (potential) into action (kinetic). The impulse of the phrase is the place where the phrase starts to work. It needs the aliveness of the *first* beat of the metric wave as well as the power of a harmonic beat for its "take-off." If the phrase starts on an up beat before the impulse, it will be played on the exhalation release from the previous phrase. A "suspended" phrase is one that starts on any beat other than the first or last beat of a measure. It will use the energy geared for the new phrase, but it will not have phrase form. It will have the feeling of leaning toward the impulse rather than one of independent authority. Its "unit" form will be that of the metric wave, melodic respiration, note-value timing and harmonic beat content.

The climax demands the tiny throb of the harmonic beat, but it can occur anywhere in the measure. There must be no leakage between the phrases, and there will not be if the phrase is filled with the content of body follow-through. Realizing the harmonic color of at least the cadential chords adds much to the content of the phrase ending. Everything after the climax is an energy exhalation breathed off completely, making ready for the inhalation on the new impulse.

SUGGESTIONS TO TEACHERS

Do not expect to know all of the Answers
Perfection is not an attainment — it is a goal

POSITION AT THE PIANO — Sit back far enough, with the lower back out, so that the diaphragm is over the leg-break and the foot arches. You are free when the whole body pivots on the center and can go in any direction according to the demands of the music and what it does to you. Your body must be in front of the playing, never behind it. "Rest down — Power up" is the feeling maintained throughout. The body texture matches the level of the music, which is the rhythmic value of the fastest note in the composition, a texture you prepare before playing begins.

FOCUS OF ATTENTION — You can consider only one aspect of the music at a time. This is the reason for the importance of making the right body responses to the musical demands habitual, so that they will not need to receive further attention. Repeat the right way at least three times, so that the home practice will become a right habit rather than a wrong one (which will have to be undone at the next lesson). Follow through with one idea until the child relates to it with a feeling-thinking self. However, if you come to an impasse, do not hesitate to change your approach, never by negation but by way of adventure.

LEARNING — Creative Motion teaches us to play from an inner necessity. For the motion way of learning the expression can be no more than the inner growth of the individual. In this way growth is a continual expansion of the individual's musicianship. Learning does not depend so much on remembering what the teacher said as remembering the "feeling" of the experience and the sound it brought forth. As far as possible let the definition come from the student. How did it feel? What was the difference in the sound? We grow through our feeling selves first, then through our action or definitional selves.

Relate your body to the composition. Is it mental with its center balance in the head arch (e.g. Chopin's Butterfly Etude, Op. 25)? Is it emotive with its balance centered at the diaphragm (e.g. Chopin's E major Etude, Op. 10)? Or is it vital, balanced at the pelvic center (e.g. Revolutionary Etude, Op. 10)? Of course there is a possible interplay of these levels. Rest on the timing, the "now" of the whole experience. The four elements of motion in all levels of approach are:

1. Rest on the arch of the hand with sprung diaphragm over it.
2. Instantaneous flight with body follow through.

3. Once further extension essential to the climactic turn-over.

4. Exhalation that covers and ensures the next impulse.

Remember that if one level of motion is improved all of the other levels are likely to become improved, for the creative motion principle is the same at all levels.

ALIVENESS — Aliveness starts at the center. When you sing music to yourself, you think and feel motion. This is the advantage of inside singing. When the inner motion is put outside, let the focus be that of the body riding the hand-arch. The light-weight-body and the breathing make the buoyancy. The body rides over the top of the readiness so that the energy force is mobilized and ready for the extraversion. The whole thing depends upon the connection between the center (light-weight-body) and the circumference, which is instantaneous to the governing idea. Rest all of yourself on the "going", the projection of the inner experience. The result is the oppositional balance of the finger-drop down and the rebound up. Practice the motion of the composition on top of the keys until the motion is more important than the keys. From the technical end, slow, definite, alive-sounding practice should be carried on, continually checking on body position, arches, arm break, and the resting of all of yourself on the piano.

TONE — Tone is never organized unless the body is over it. To keep tone in the keys the body with its weight balances moves along with the movement of the song. Surface tone is white and chalky with tonal leakage. "Quality" tone has depth, content, and rhythmic and tonal relationships. Depth comes from the further extension into the key bed which, in turn, ensures the flight. Content comes from the body follow through in all of its aspects, as if it were sharing the experience of the motion with the music. Holding a finger down deeper into the key until its climax, plus arch cover cures leakage. One does not lift the fingers out of the keys, the rebound from the once further finger pressure sends them to cover the next note. The rebound takes place by way of the arch, never by muscular lifting of the hand or arm. Lightness is never achieved by pulling oneself away from the tone, but by changing balances in relation to the music. Stay close to the keys, springing whatever the energy flight allows. But energy goes directly to its destination; there is economy in its flight.

IMAGERY — Imagery is the most miraculous tool of all. The governing idea of *Mind* gives way to that of the *Subconscious,* the memory of past experiences buried deep in the self-nether-world. The "take-off" of an aeroplane, the jerk of a fish on the hook, the smell of burning leaves in October, the taste of lemon juice, "my dog who never came back home"; they are all part of the deep-down self which everyone possesses. In the flash of a moment, the skillfull teacher suggests an image that "makes all of the difference" in the child's playing. It is the inside of the subconscious coming into expression for a precious moment. If once tapped, these forgotten memories well up as effortless, distilled beauty, a symbol of the most intimate, centered thing man knows, the governing idea of the subconscious mind. So use *Imagery* as the last touch of *Creative Motion.*

SOME SUGGESTIONS ON ANALYSIS

A word has no meaning unless there is experience behind it. A word becomes a symbol for reality, a re-experiencing fore-shortened for ease of time and communication.

So notes have no meaning unless experience is behind them — the body in motion in a musical world of feeling and thinking. The use of symbolic markings added to that of the notes is to communicate briefly the tonal and rhythmic effects implicit in the music which the composer intended. The symbol is the outward evidence of the composite forces underlying the music. However, unless the symbol has its equivalence in an inner creative response, it will serve only an artificial purpose — a loud-soft, fast-slow series of reactions, which of themselves are not deeply pertinent.

One must always remember that the two loops of the creative spiral, feeling and action, are the fore-runners of the symbol, never the other way around. For this reason the ability to analyze music does not begin as an outside process; it always comes by way of motion at the center, by inside singing and energy extension where the response to the musical demands spring true.

"Why" and "what" and "how" are the words that stimulate the need and use of the symbol. What is the extent of the phrase; where is its climactic turn-over? What is the duration of a specific harmonic structure? What mood is created when the composer repeats again and again the tonic tone in the base, allowing no vitality of harmonic beat intervals, particularly when these repetitional notes underlie the dominant of the subdominant chord?

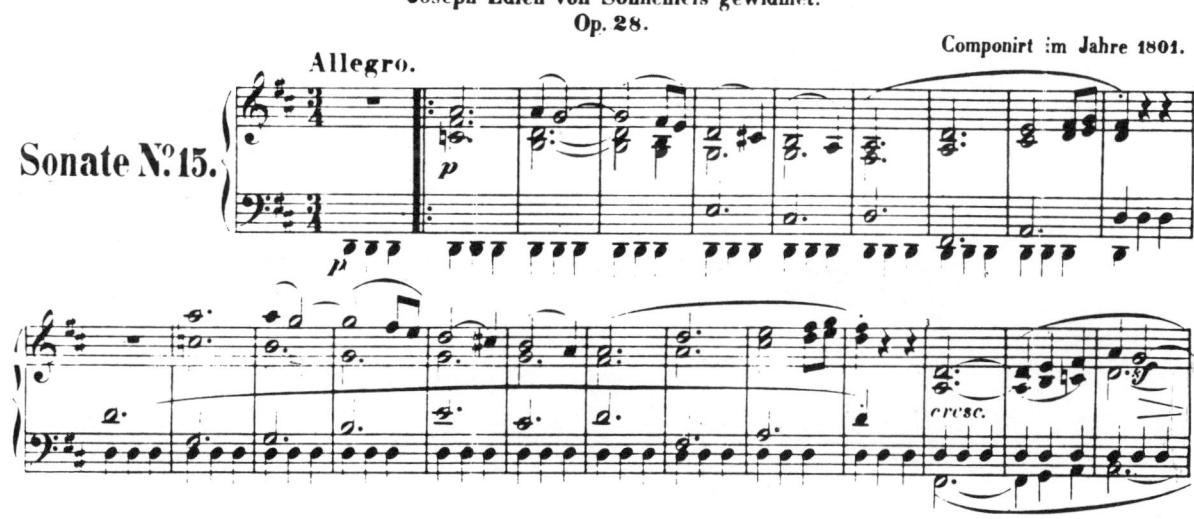

What shift in dynamics is implied when single melody tones are shifted to an octave passage? The answer to all of these questions and many more are within the orbit of symbol suggesting, as best they may, the language of the music. Analyzing is a co-creation, an experience of becoming, witnessing the birth of the music.

Creative motion analysis does not disregard in any way the markings of the composer as found in reliable publications. If anything, the creative motion teacher watches them with even more interest than one might otherwise, since again and again the dynamic markings on a manuscript coincide with the effects evidenced by the creative motion symbol.

Beethoven in his F sharp major Sonata, Opus 78, Number 24, measures 7 and 8 uses a crescendo leading up to the high point of the phrase with a decrescendo on through its cadence. In Creative Motion we would not only analyze it as a phrase of 5 (as the Beethoven crescendo indicates) but we would also be sentient to the shift from lateral to vertical on the climax as well as the return from the subdominant to the tonic over a sustained reiteration of the #F harmonic beat. These factors will make the climax less out-going than as if the melody ascended to another lateral tone, or as if it moved to any chord other than the tonic. None of these relationships are suggested by the ⎯⎯⎯⎯⎯⎯⎯⎯ but each is basic to the awareness and expression of this phrase.

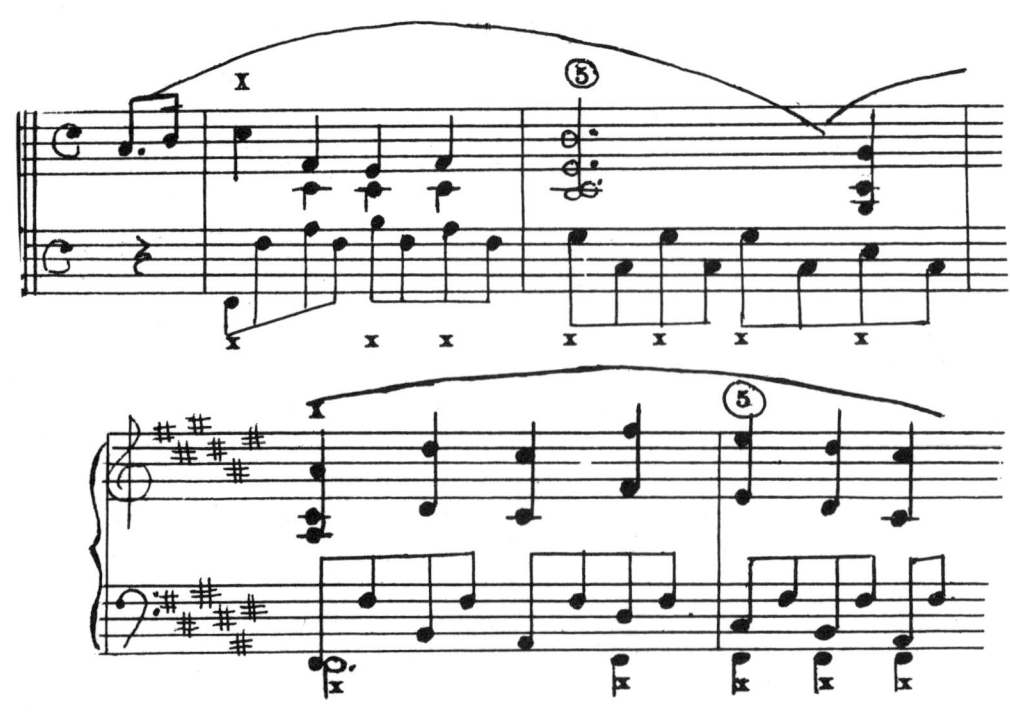

100

A crescendo or increase of sound is not identical with the extension produced by the energy rebound of the impulse going to the climax with its release of energy for the cadence. It might be the same if expressed by a gifted person who relates intuitively the musical demands to the energy pattern (as seen in the yawn). If so, the listening world would name it a great moment of music, experienced through the medium of a person of great talent. (After one of Yehudi Menuhim's gloriously convincing concerts, I asked him the secret of his musical vibrancy. He looked me straight in the eye and said: "I breath for every phrase.") But the usual music student would not be by nature so sensitive; he would increase his power for the crescendo and decrease it as the symbol suggests. But the extraverted action of loud to soft does not have within it the phrase extension which inevitably brings the climactic turn-over, the very quality that gives the phrase its final release of energy for the cadence. Try it both ways and see how different each feels and how different each sounds. The crescendo and decrescendo are in evidence, not because they are muscularly willed, but rather because they are the inevitable result of the tonal growth of this phrase.

A composer's symbols for dramatic tensions: the ffs, sf, $>$ pps, are part of our musical heritage and should be observed if we strive to recapture the composer's dramatic quality. However, scholars of music point out that composers are not always consistent in their markings. In such instances the teacher must test and retest the motion of the music through his own inner experience in order to make as valid an analysis of which he is capable. Of course, one may not be able always to decide on a fixed and exact analysis. One's feelings as to the composer's intentions may vary from time to time. And, as one may differ with oneself, one may differ with others. This flexibility is not a weakness of creative motion: it is a strength. Music must remain open to different interpretations to retain its aliveness as an art. Regardless of the outcome, the struggle to decide between various meanings will assure a more vibrant, more interesting interpretation than if one makes no motion analysis at all.

From the beginning of this section of the book, analysis has been a step-by-step process. The symbols designated below are just a final part of the analysis. They are simple, only a meager suggestion. They do not indicate one idea, a single experience in mind, but rather they express the feeling-action loops of the creative spiral. They arouse an awareness-feeling along with an outside response which allows that feeling an extraverted expression.

SYMBOLS:
    X placed below each harmonic beat.
    L for lateral, V for vertical, placed above the top tone of the harmonic beat to observe the
        melodic respiration.
    An arc drawn over the notes showing the extent of the phrase.
    X placed above each phrase impulse.
    0 for the phrase climax. The phrase shape number drawn within the circle.
    The symbols for the harmonic color content are those used for the triads, i.e. I, IV, V, etc.

The symbols are chosen according to the needs of the music and the needs of the student. All previous editorial markings and fingering have been removed in order to clarify the creative motion symbols. The teacher will, of course, have his personal copy for use as reference and comparison.

This is the reason for analysis: to study the creative form so carefully that you can communicate its meaning, as nearly as possible, to those who wish to hear and know.

MINUET   BACH

The body is geared to the fastest note in the composition, which determines the torso balance over the thighs (see chart No. 1, Page 46). The music is centered around this bodily balance.

In choosing the dramatic level (mental, emotive, or vital) we get the over all feel of the music. This minuet is mental, finely edged with delicate grace. The bass notes make a melodic pattern, each note of equal importance in the design, hence they are all harmonic beats.

The top notes of the harmonic beats are circled to indicate the melodic respiration. The uncircled notes flow out of the preceding harmonic beat on its way to the next harmonic beat. Use the words "lateral" (up in pitch) or "vertical" (down in pitch) as you sing these notes, realizing the direction of the melodic respiration. The harmonic beats (including the melodic respiration) will be played off of the back hand arch. All of the other notes will come off of the anterior arch. In this Minuet this observation is of great importance; it makes all of the difference in the musical result. In measure 1, only G and A are melodic respiration notes; the other melody notes do not ascend on the tonic chord with the power of the back arch. They ride the arc of the harmonic beat flight after the pulse has been expressed. (This measure is rarely played correctly.)

Since the B section moves to the relative minor, the student should get a minor quality in the music by feeling a slight lowering of the diaphragmatic center. This will ensure a minor quality. The harmonic content is simple, only I, IV and V chords are used. The student and teacher should take time to hear-feel the chords throughout.

The well balanced phrases are those of four and seven, authentic minuet phrasing. Their shape gives gentle grace and flow to the dance as well as high-lighting the round metre of 3. The energy extension from impulse to climax must be experienced on every phrase; however, with such short, orderly phrases, the lung breath and energy breath can move together. This helps to make more real the turn-over of power on the climax as well as the release of energy on the cadence.

Minuet

ALLEGRO from the SONATINA No. 1   CLEMENTI

This Allegro movement of the Clementi Sonatina might well be renamed: "a study in harmonic beat structure." One could hardly find a better example. It uses every value of harmonic beat duration: whole note, dotted half, half, quarter, and eighth. It is written in cut time: the note value symbols remain the same as in 4/4 time. The ¢ measure has only two beats instead of four, the metric wave motion thrusts immediately to the second beat, the climax of the measure. (The flight of energy of the metric wave in 4/4 also covers immediately the climax of the measure. However, the follow-through of the metric beat timing allows four beats rather than two.) The over all body stance would register for the 𝅗𝅥 balance in the cut time rather than 𝅘𝅥 for 4/4 time. The body will be geared to the fastest note 𝅘𝅥𝅮 balanced over the 𝅘𝅥𝅮 part of the thigh. It is written on the mental level which demands fine articulation, edged with precision.

From former comments on harmonic beats, you will remember that the harmonic beat pulse springs with sufficient energy to carry over to the following harmonic beat; however, it is played with the balance designated by its particular note value. In the first measure there is only one harmonic beat, but its complete flight in ¢ takes two counts with its climax on the second count. The second measure repeats this same design; the third has two harmonic beats, each absorbing one count for its flight. In measure four the harmonic beat flight is completed in one count. The following four descending 𝅘𝅥𝅮 notes form a bass melody. Each note is of equal importance, therefore making all of them harmonic beats. In measure nine there is an Alberti bass allowing two harmonic beats, each with a flight of one count.

Thus the music moves on easily enough with unquestionable clarity until one comes to measure five of Section B. The question is whether each bass note is a harmonic beat; or, do we follow the bass Melody line formed by the first and third notes of each measure 20 through 23, f-d-e♭c-b♮-c-g-low g? With the many repeated g's in the right hand, the g in the bass, if given the importance of a harmonic beat, becomes exaggerated and over-bearing. If analyzed as we suggest above, the bass melody relieves the over repetition of the g's. If the interpreter feels the need for the dominant emphasis, he may prefer to make each note a harmonic beat.

The student should feel by experiencing the suggested harmonic beat markings, letting the diaphragm spring the motion, with the arm and pencil-in-hand following (never with muscular pushing). He should sing the melody as he follows this motion before he begins to play any notes. Beginning in this manner is imperative since the right hand might absorb all of the aural attention, subsequently disregarding the harmonic beat flight upon which the melody actually moves. If the harmonic beat arc of motion, as it is drawn on the musical manuscript, is really felt, the second beat (cut time) will become the "over-the-top" extension and climax, even though the tone comes down in pitch. The climax of the measure and that of the harmonic beat are simultaneous.

Phrase form usually falls easily into shape after studying the harmonic beat structure. Each is contigent upon the other. So let us look at the phrasing. There is a rule of thumb that says: if a motive is repeated it becomes two phrases. This is not always true, but give it a chance in analyzation. The first two measures of the Clementi sonatina are an example in question. Do we have two phrases of one each, or is it a phrase flight of longer duration? If there were a change of harmony on the second measure, the music would indicate a longer phrase. But in this case, if the second harmonic beat is harmonically identical with the first, I believe that they form two phrases of one each, with its

tiny explosion of the impulse and climax being released together. Measures five and six, and also measures twenty-eight and twenty-nine, might at first appear to be phrases of one. However, they are not exactly identical, and the force exerted by the octave leap of C in the bass binds the two measures together in a phrase of 3 in both instances.

Returning to the analyzation of the harmonic beat, the color content of the chord structure of the B Section modulates to the minor. Here the music demands a lowered diaphragmatic balance, thus assuring a minor quality.

Clementi uses only the simple fundamental chords: I, IV, V, and their inversions — all of which should be known and felt by the serious student, particularly on the last five measures, which serve as the climax of the entire movement of this delightful sonatina.

BOURREE FROM THE SECOND VIOLIN SONATA   Bach

Comparing the original edition of Bach's Second violin Sonata with the piano version transcribed from it, we see that the basic harmonic beat structure of the latter has been taken almost literally from Bach's original plan. There are existing harmonic beats to serve the necessities of the phrase structure throughout. The music is direct and strong, created on the vital level, centering the power in the torso area. Both are written in cut time which changes the usual phrase shape of 5 in 4/4 time to that of 3 in 2/4 time; however, felt from the vital level, the phrase motion has great vitality. The cut meter gives the Bourree an ever advancing swing.

Although a bourree is a simple dance form, Bach, in the original violin sonata, gives the third, fourth, and fifth phrase an unexpected shift in shape. In the first two of these irregular phrases, rather than continuing a phrase of 3, which he has already given two times, he omits the harmonic beat on the first beat of the measure, thus eliminating the chance of an impulse, and puts it on the first beat of the second measure with the impulse and climax together in a phrase of 1. This same structure is adhered to in the piano transcript. In the original edition, the impulse of the third of these irregular phrases is held over until the second measure where the first beat is qualified as an impulse because of its harmonic structure. It forms a phrase of 5. Here the piano transcript departs from the form of the violin score. There is a harmonic beat directly after the anacrusis which allows this first beat of a phrase to become an impulse, thus making it a phrase of 7. The inside-feeling-motion substantiates this analysis, and when played according to the musical demands, although not identical, these 3 phrases not only give suspense and tension to the Bourree, but the delight of phrase contrast. Do not pass them unobserved, as they so often are.

The fifth phrase, according to the piano version, could have its climax on either the first beat of the third or fourth measures, making it either a phrase of 5 or 7. However, if we look at the original score we see that there is no harmonic beat on the high A directly after the ascending eighth note run. (Measure 11) If we take a cue from the earlier Bach, we will feel it as a phrase of 7 rather than one of 5. The vitality of this longer phrase is echoed in the following short phrase of 1. After another phrase of 3, we come to the phrase whose analysis is the most difficult and crucial to determine. In the piano transcript, the choice could be either the phrase of 7 or 9. If the climax comes on the last B flat major chord, it will take an amazing amount of energy extension to go that far before the climactic release. On the other hand, if we choose the preceding B flat major chord in the first inversion for the climax, we might question it because of the octave exuberance that issues out of this climax. However, the octaves are all descending on a vertical line of motion, on an exhalation of energy. In this way the last three measures become a dramatic explosion of released energy, a defined cadence on a brilliant exhalation. After offering supporting reasons for each of these choices in the piano transcription, we look at the original Bach and find that the longer phrase of 9 is the only possible one since the note just before the descending eighth note run where the phrase of 7 would be climaxed, is not a harmonic beat; therefore, our choice is determined if we go to the original Bach for our decision. Our energy extension will continue further and further, almost to the breaking point, until the climactic turn over and its release of energy on the final dramatic chord of I.

Tempo di Bourrée.

Bourrée.
(From the Second Violin-Sonata.)

Allegro.

16.

BAGATELLE Mozart

In analyzing 6/8 metric motion, there are two basic beats each absorbing three counts. The phrase shape will be determined by counting two beats to a measure.

A student should always envision a "red light" outside of a 6/8 signature so that he will stop long enough to realize that the music is not in 3/4 time; 6/8 is a totally different motion combining square and round rhythm, with its two sets of three eighth notes. I believe this oversight or lack of inner relationship to the rhythmic demands of 6/8 rhythm is the most prevalent one in music training; yet, it is the most beautiful motion that music offers: a curve of power with the climax on the 4th beat. To incorporate this feeling in the analysis, let the rebound of the impulse ride over the inarticulate second and third beats to tip-touch the climax of 4 on its return to the impulse of the next measure. I have rarely heard 6/8 motion have the quality of motion that makes of it such a beautiful experience. Once a composition in 6/8 metre is partially learned, it is wise to change the count of six to that of the two basic pulses, therefore making it easier to feel the second beat high as the climax of the measure on its way to the next impulse, rather than moving through the six successive numbers.

The Bagatelle lends itself particularly well to further experience with melodic respiration. As you remember from the previous section on harmonic beat structure: when you spring "down-up" on a harmonic beat, the energy registers either "wide" or "tall" according to the pitch movement of the melody. The body shifts its balance in response to the lateral-vertical motion of the melody. It is the shifts in the energy respiration that brings about the related body response.

The melodic respiration or melody tones of the harmonic beat for the first six measures are as follows:

>Wide, wide, tall
>Wide, wide, more wide
>Tall, tall, more tall, wide, tall, tall
>wide, wide, tall
>Wide, wide, more wide
>Tall, tall, tall, wide, tall

This allows the melody to breathe. To respond to the melodic respiration serves as a guide to the dynamics which are incipient in the melody and harmonic structure when they were created. The more the student and teacher relate to the melodic respiration, the more fluid the music becomes. The tensions and releases feel truer because the melodic respiration is based on the out-go and in-go of energy as it registers in relation to the musical flow. The melody, in turn, is the outside edge of the throb made manifest by the union of the tones of the triad.

BAGATELLE

W. A. MOZART

LASCIA CH'IO PIANGA (Let Me Weep)   Handel

The art of accompanying adds another dimension to a musical experience in which one relates not only individually to the music, but also one in which the accompanist encompases with equal concern the singer's musical sensitivity. The following suggestions should be kept in mind when accompanying: (1) The text must be as familiar to the pianist as to the vocalist, not just the words, but also the inner meaning of the words which eventually radiate through the tonal medium. (2) The breathing of the singer, the combination of his lung breath and energy breath, must become familiar to the accompanist so that the same response is felt simultaneously by both. It is the awareness of these respirations that allows the accompanist and soloist to ride on top of the music, to feel the phrase flight with its controlled extension of power. (3) As Lotte Lehman says: "I sing with every cell in my body." So a singer uses his body to support the various gradations of feeling which the music demands. Power, delicate nuance, hesitant indecision, directed and accelerated purpose — these and many more are a part of the energy modulations which the singer has at his command. The pianist must sense in advance these subtle changes, experiencing them as sincerely as the soloist if the two are to become one in feeling and artistic projection.

Often the more simple the accompaniment, the more difficult it is to keep the musical unity between the two musicians. For this reason I have chosen the aria, "Lascia ch'io pianga," from Handel's opera, *Rinaldo,* which, in the Handel-Gesellschaft edition, is simplicity itself. There are no frills or tonal escapades to hide behind: every note is laid out in the open, pure and clear; the harmonic progressions cluster around the basic chord structures. Here is a classic lament not only in the anguished poetry of the words, but in the feeling content of the music:

ARIA   Let me weep my cruel fate,
And let me breathe freedom!
Let sorrow break these chains
Of my sufferings, for pity's sake.

A danger signal might be implied by the repetition of the chords in the first two measures. If the pianist is unaware of this repetition, and if the chords are played with no inner motion, they more than likely will become weighted and static. If the second chord is on the same level as the first, the rhythmic and phrase motion will be lost and may never be regained. The assured protection against this hazard is to feel the motion of the metric wave within the measure containing the repetition. If the body realizes this arc-of-the-wave motion, no one of the repeated chords will sound alike; it will portray in sound a going away and a return. Pulse and breath off for each of several measures of 3/4 time, being aware of the climactic turn over on the last half of the second beat. As you do so, think the note values of these particular measures until the metric wave moves freely. As soon as possible the metric wave motion should be absorbed by the larger experience of phrase motion.

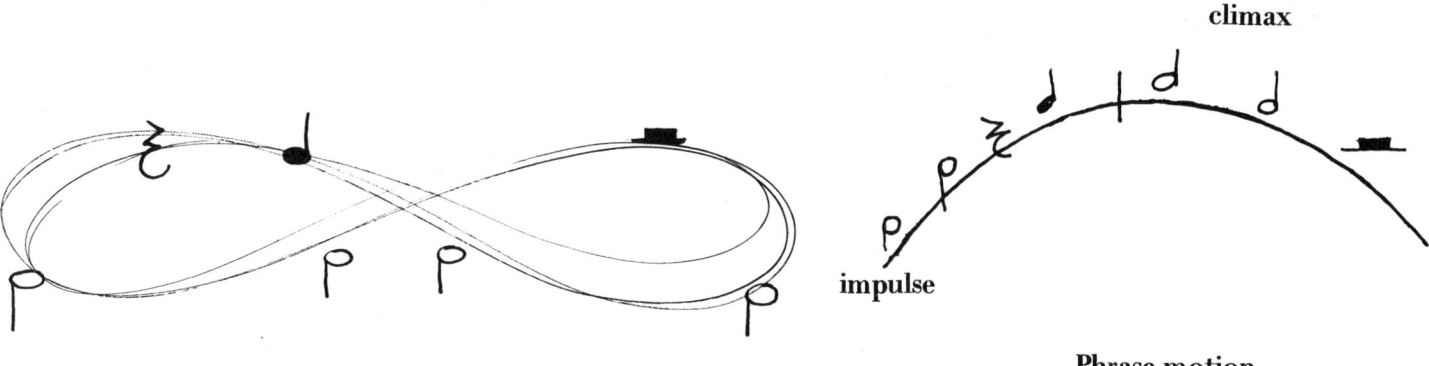

Phrase motion

Only two times in the first fourteen measures is the climax of the measure tonally articulated and then only by a receding bass note at the end of measures 4 and 14. All of the other measure climaxes are little "sighs" of stricken grief.

The melody starts on the tone of the third as we might expect in so tender a song. After two short phrases of 4, subdued and introspective, Handel gives a phrase of 7. Here the melody rises one note above the high F with a new sense of freedom only to rest down again on the tone of the third for its climax on the first syllable of the word, "liberta."

Every bass note is a harmonic beat. The "lateral" and "vertical" of the harmonic respiration breathes gently over the harmonic beat structure. The color content of the chords is easy to follow and adds much to the harmonic flow and feeling.

This is Handel in one of his epic moments. As an aria it has limited chance to be known by the usual piano student. This is a case in favor of a worthy transcription. The following one was printed by the Presser Publishing Company several years ago. It stands on its own merits as an unspoiled transcription. The phrasing is identical with that of the Gesellschaft edition.

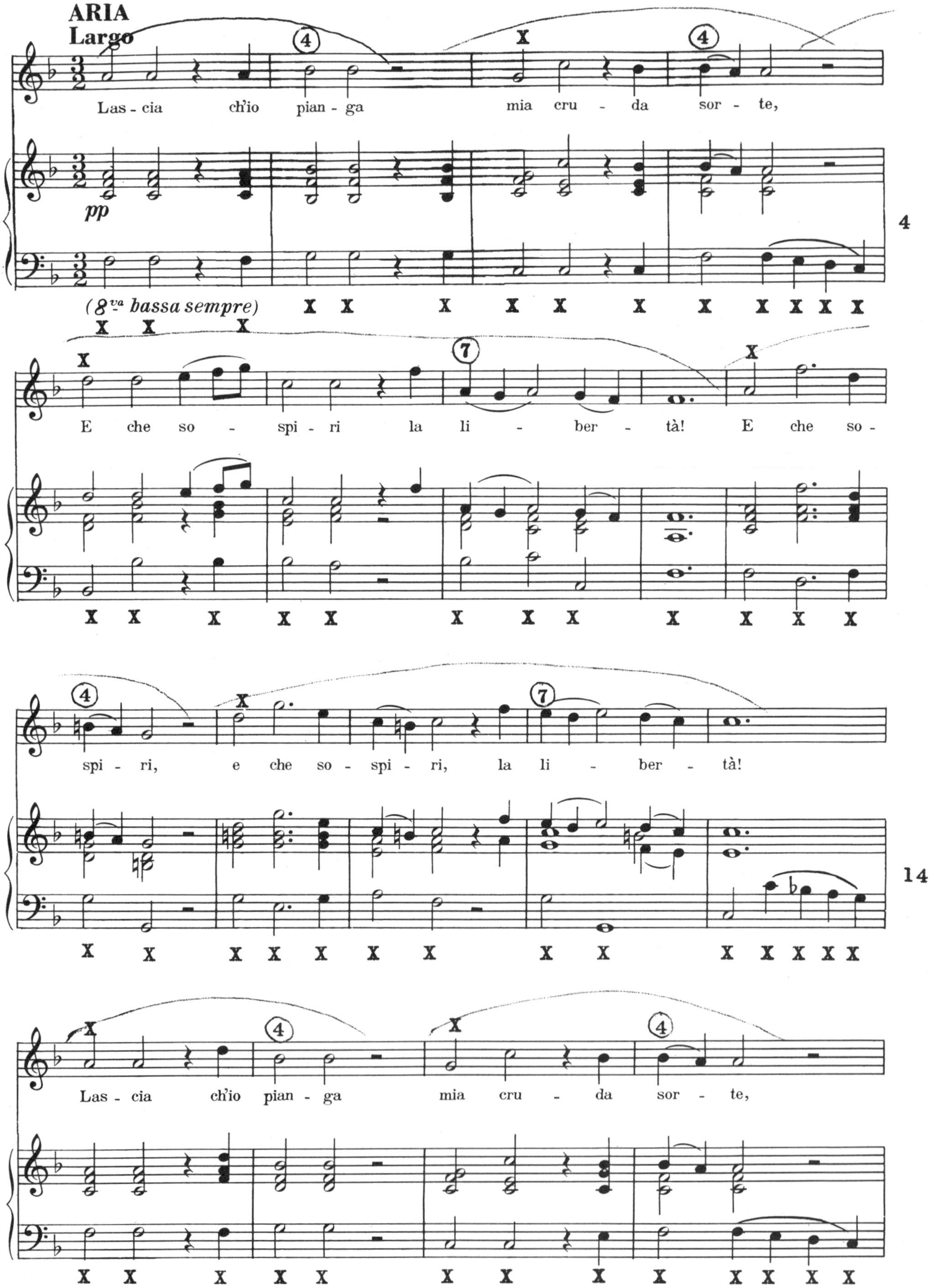
ARIA
Largo
(8va bassa sempre)
pp
Las - cia ch'io pian - ga mia cru - da sor - te,
E che so - spi - ri la li - ber - tà! E che so -
spi - ri, e che so - spi - ri, la li - ber - tà!
Las - cia ch'io pian - ga mia cru - da sor - te,
4
14

LET ME WEEP.
Lascia Ch'io Pianga.

G. F. HÄNDEL.

MENUETTO from the SONATA in E flat Major   Opus 31, No. 3   Beethoven

After careful attempts at analyzing, it is not always easy to discover the composer's intended phrase form. As one conscientious teacher said: "In the morning I am certain that in this Menuetto there are two phrases of four at the beginning. By night I feel that there is only one long phrase of seven". Under certain circumstances such shifts may be a sign of versatility, not one of inconsistancy, in both the music and the musical analyst. The interest, the curiosity, the effort, the questioning are the real reward.

Beethoven's Menuetto is an example to prove the previous statement. The first eight measures might be done in several ways, combining various phrase lengths. I have indicated on the music manuscript two possible phrase lengths. Do not look at them just with your eyes. See the phrase as you relate it to your incoming and outgoing breath, or as you relate it to your inside singing. In such instances as this, the way that finally feels the most comfortable can be your choice.

There is not such leeway in determining the harmonic beat structure; at the first glance its meaning is often hidden. Here in the B section of the Menuetto we find such a quandary. How many notes fall out of the low B flat harmonic beat? Are all of the notes harmonic beats? Are only the repeated B flats the beats? Or is there a hidden independent melody in the bass voice that might give the clue? As you ponder these questions let us look at the upper voice in the first two measures of the B section. Here is a melody line that becomes in the second measure an alto descant. Here Beethoven has definitely made the notes appear important by changing their metric value. The bass notes directly under this alto melody form a duet in which each line is of equal importance. In the last phrase in this section the bass melody becomes increasingly active, moving with virility on to the final cadence. Each note of this bass melody is a harmonic beat. Test this analysis with your pedal. See if it pleases your ear, and feels true to the motion principles. These are two ways of knowing if you are meeting the demands of the music.

TRIO

The Trio is a virile contrast to the gracious curves of the Menuetto. The interval leaps indicate a shift from the emotive to the vital level. The harmonic beats demand exciting cover. The come-off for the staccato notes is the result of the very first impact with the keys. The arm-break then carries the hand (with the arch leading the direction of the motion) across the interval expanse. As the half note chord is being held a "once-further" into the keys will ensure the rebound. In the phrase of seven on the second line, using the metric wave helps to put form into the continued repetition of the diminished seventh chord.

THREE PRELUDES OF CHOPIN
A MAJOR, Opus 28, No. 7

This prelude is a fine example of the hierarchy of phrase level. A simple pattern is repeated, and by the rule of thumb (suggested at the beginning of this chapter) each complete design repeated becomes a phrase. But in this instance, two of the smaller phrases of 4 join and make a longer phrase of 7. A pattern, twice as long as the original one, will still be repeated. This interpretation has an argument in its favor: that the climax now comes on a harmonic change with its impact of color content which makes the climactic turn-over easier to fulfill. The widening extension from impulse to climax and the exhalation release now have become the respiration wave that gives this simple prelude its flowing charm.

Since the harmonic beat pulse supplies sufficient energy to carry through two measures rather than the traditional one, this A major prelude becomes a modified form of a waltz. The harmonic beats extend through six counts rather than the usual three. The only exceptions are in measures 12 and 14 in which new harmonies develop, each of which necessitates a tiny harmonic beat pulse. As we know from experience, harmonic beats spring first at the diaphragmatic center and from there move out to the other arches by way of radiant coordination. The harmonic balances in the leg and foot are in rapport with those of the arm and hand. Consequently the foot and hand arch will automatically join together in the harmonic pulse with the rare exceptions indicated by a blurred melodic line. The pedal may be held down six counts interrupted slightly by a pedal release to clear the close intervals of the ♩. ♪ . The alteration of the waltz rhythm, as found in the 12th and 14th measures, will determine the pedal response accordingly (with the help of the ear).

The climax of the entire prelude, toward which each tone has been moving, is the final defined cadence chord of the third phrase: the dominant seventh of the supertonic. For a fleeting moment the prelude is lit with a tense brilliance, only to give way to a minor shadow before leading back to the cool calm of arrival.

*This could be considered a harmonic beat if the II^7 chord were considered a separate entity from that of the II, otherwise there would be just one harmonic beat to this measure.

C MINOR PRELUDE, Opus 28, No. 20.

There are times when a wise teacher analyzes a composition for its likely technical hurdles before the lesson begins. Such procedure bears witness to the adage: "A stitch in time saves nine". Practicing the wrong way for a week establishes almost indelible habits which might otherwise have been prevented. I believe that the C minor prelude is a good example for such anticipated concern.

Three prevalent hurdles come to my mind: lack of rebound, surface playing which makes for white chalky tone, and careless response to timing and cover.

1 – Lack of rebound is prevalent in a largo tempo such as this one. The rebound of the harmonic beat feels delayed, and, as a result might be disregarded altogether. A rebound that sends one to the next tonal articulation is a turning of force because of the hand pressure against the keybed resistance. The pressure down must be a constant, growing experience. There is no moment in which one relaxes into indifference. In a slow tempo, counting "and" between each beat may help. The rebound comes on the "and" at which time the hand arches and arms are sent by a force, seemingly outside of oneself, with economy of motion, gliding along just above the surface of the keys. Immediately the harmonic beats will take on vitality and strength.

2 – If the student has realized the responsibility stated in the first paragraph, our second hurdle has been partially jumped over. Going deeper and deeper into the keybed will help to counteract surface playing. However responding to the color content of the chords will greatly enrich the irredescent quality of tonal relationships. The chords in the first phrase: I, IV, V, and I involve the player in the basic emotive reactions: security, desire, action and arrival. These same harmonies are repeated in the submediant, played with a lifted diaphragm because of the shift to the major mode. Continue this harmonic concern throughout the prelude. Finally become aware of and respond to the melodic respiration so that the melody flows with the interplay of the lateral and vertical line.

3 – The ♩. ♬ figure played over the quarter note octave in the bass needs to be visualized as synchronized motion. The left hand holds its octave until the climax of the note (half its metrical value). Exactly on the dot the left hand prepares the following octave on a rebound by moving directly over it. The right hand will anticipate the sixteenth note by the adjustment of hand balance, but it will not be played until after the left hand is poised over the octave harmonic beat about to be played. If the student waits to prepare the octave in the left hand as he plays the sixteenth note, the timing will never be right, nor will the sixteenth note fall into place on the following chord with the delicacy and grace it rightfully possesses.

The phrasing of the second line shows a possible shift in the phrase length. Here the tonal dictates of the bass overule the power of the repeated rhythmic design, thus creating a phrase of five. In the third measure the bass voice, forming couplets closed in by similar intervals, and using the strong harmonic sequence I, IV, V, I, returns again to a phrase of three. The fourth measure, using the chord of the sixth as the related tonic (reflecting its use from the second measure of the prelude) repeats the harmonic action of the previous measure, thus creating another phrase of three. But Chopin adds one more tonic chord, an octave higher, with its final assurance breathed through a lateral expanse.

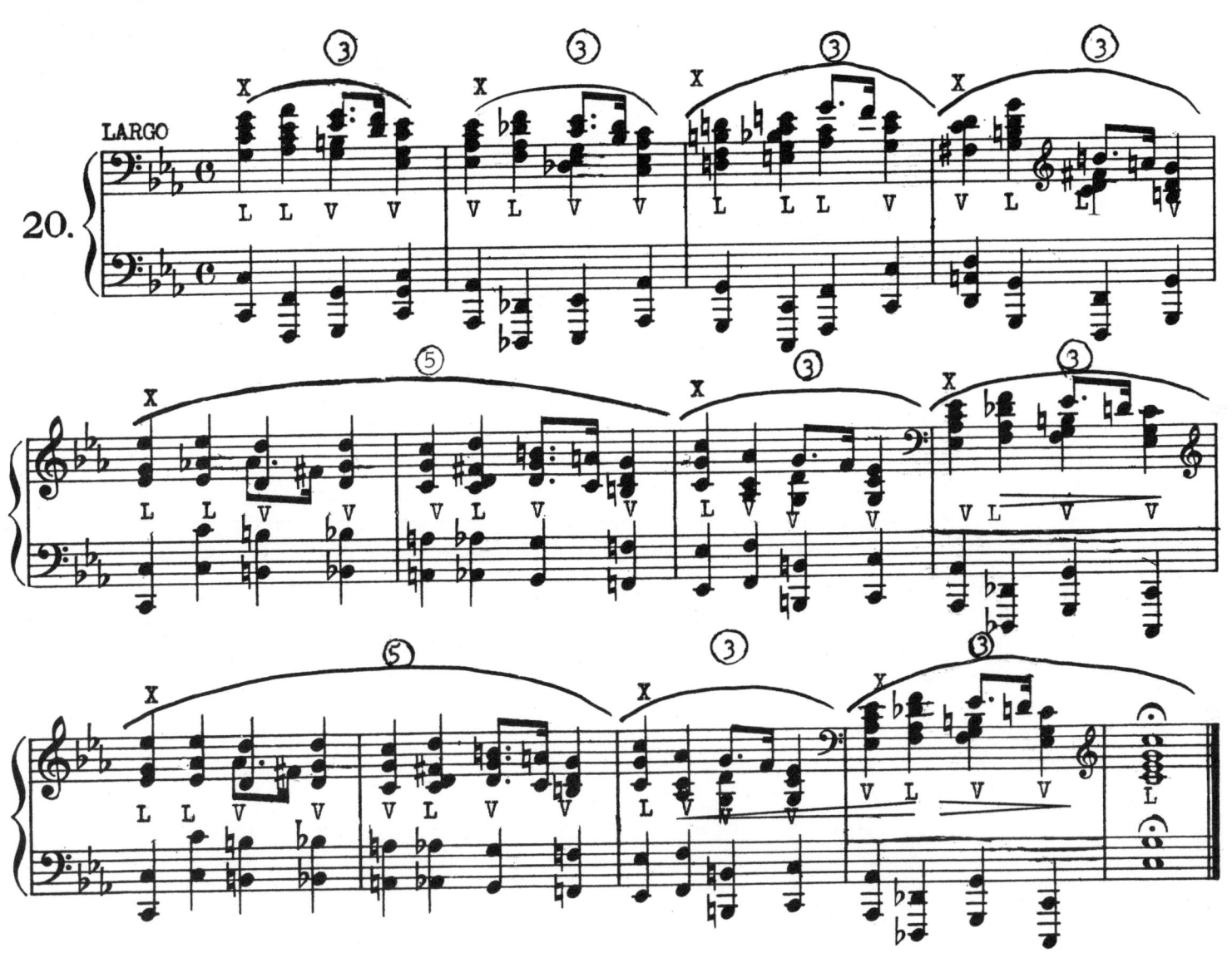

B MINOR PRELUDE, Opus 28, No. 6

This prelude could be distinguished by its division between the lateral and vertical lines of motion. In the first half (measures 1 to 15) wherever the figure ♪♪♪♪ appears it always ascends; from measures 16 to 24 it always descends. ♪♪♪♪ The last phrase is a repetition of the first phrase of the prelude, as if to bind together the beginning and the end in a circle of wholeness. The low B on the last impulse is tied to the previous low B to make the illusion of connection all the greater.

Each one of the bass melody notes is a harmonic beat. We not only hear them throb with life, but if we listen carefully we become aware of energy patterns which compensate for the space to be covered. The first sixteenth note grouping ascends to the third above the octave; the second figure releases enough energy to ascend beyond the tone of the third to that of the fifth; the third phrase foregoes the tonic root and starts the figure on low G with sufficient force to mount up two octaves. Having done so, the bass melody continues with harmonic changes on every eighth note as if it were carrying an important message with agitation and resolve. In measures 13 and 14 the C major arpeggio is used twice in succession. It does not serve, however, as a true repeat, for the phrase shape varies. The first low C is an impulse and climax together forming a phrase of I, the following low C begins the upbeat bridging over to the E above middle C, serving as an impulse and climax in a phrase of 1. These last mentioned phrases may be the climax of the entire prelude; from now on all of the motion descends. Only the deceptive cadence is lit with courage, but just for a brief moment. From then on the bass harmonic beat melody takes us further and further down to its inevitable end.

I have said nothing about the right hand. Only the notes directly over the bass notes are part of the harmonic beat, and as such will spring simultaneously with the left hand. All of the other notes fall out of the anterior arch on the way to the next harmonic beat. The repeated notes will not sound identical: the second note of a repeated series will be played off of a more lifted arch, and consequently will sound like an echo, faint and far away.

ROMANCE F sharp major. OP. 28 no. 2 SCHUMANN

Recently a musician colleague, whose sensitive evaluation of music I regard very highly, said to me, "Why is it that Schumann's F sharp Major Romance is rarely played well, or with the depth of color and emotion I am convinced that Schumann created?"

This is the sort of question that becomes an active challenge to a searching-out music student: his vigor is sparked to discover by hearing-feeling-thinking the enigma that lies beneath the welter of notes laid out before him. I suggested to my friendly critic that we approach the Romance in the light of Creative Motion, to study its form and content by applying the principles of creativity. This we did. I include it as an ending in this section of the book, for the Romance unites the obvious with the deeply hidden, the evident assurance with the doubt, the puzzling question which Creative Motion helps to solve.

Let us look first at the harmonic beat structure. The usual rule being that the lowest note of a harmonic group is the note that releases the harmonic energy, all of the secondary notes emerge out of this harmonic throb. However, the lowest note in each harmonic group for the first four measures (f sharp) falls on either a weak beat of the measure or an off beat. The same structure prevails for the next four measures, using various low notes, so that in none of these first eight measures does a lowest note sound on a first beat. Applying the usual rule for harmonic beat brings the difficulty that there can be no phrase impulse — since an impulse must be a harmonic beat on the first beat — until measure nine. Can there be another solution?

The bass voice, however, participates in the duet-like melody between the two inner voices. Together these two voices represent an independent duet melody, the notes of which form the harmonic beat structure. The independent melody takes precedence here over the usual rule that the lowest note of a broken chord series is the harmonic beat. (The same holds true for the return of the opening theme in measure 18.)

The harmonic beats of section B, by contrast, are on the octaves in the bass voice, which contribute strength and directness; but see how close the intervals are in this bass line, symbolizing strength of purpose, but not with the daring quality of a larger interval. In this B section, the impulse of the first phrase is on G sharp minor, (a related II of the original tonality, with its tension). The impulse of the second phrase (two measures later) uses a 7th chord on the sixth degree. The diaphragm crumples beneath the introverted remorse of this harmonic moment.

In 6/8 time the basic motion is felt as two beats to a measure. The phrase shape is dependent upon the length of time between the impulse and the climax formed by the crest of the extension. Any specific phrase shape depends upon the amount of released energy of the impulse. In this composition we have phrase lengths of 3, 4, 6, 2 and 1, each bearing a direct relationship not only to the same tones on the diatonic series, but also to the harmonic feeling of the triads III, IV, VI, II and I. It may be a paradox, but music experienced and analyzed through the body medium proves this relationship again and again: III with its emotive color, the unifying factor between the first and fifth tones of the scale; IV with desire coupled with reticent action; VI with its feeling of almost pregnant abundance; II a dissonance that thrives on tension; I the final security and serenity of arrival.

In looking back over the phrase structure of the A section we discover that the climax of the two phrases of 2 (measure 5 and 6) amazingly enough come on the lowest note of the harmonic series for the first time. But Schumann, in his genius way, chose to tie both the upper and lower duet-melody voices of the harmonic beat which puts them for a moment into the shadow, so that the low G sharp and F sharp sings out with greater evidence. Realizing the inner motion of these two climaxes gives a particular deep-seated and subtle pleasure because the lowest note, which previously had been deprived of harmonic power, becomes a harmonic beat on the crest of the climax!

In the last section (measure 25) there are two phrases which use a contrapuntal conversational device. The first phrase ends with three chords leading to a diminished 7th, with its accompanying physical tension, almost an agony. The second phrase starts with an imitation of the contrapuntal device, but this time Schumann adds the strength of tonal unison that gives rise to the climax of the whole composition. The unison also leads back to the tonic, which assures the ending.

On the phrase of ① at the very end of the song, there is just a tiny puff of an energy release with the top note of the harmonic beat singing the tone of the third. May we, at the end of this Romance, call it our tone of "love"? All that remains is an echo of the motive using the first three notes of the scale, sustaining the tone of the third. The last two measures are but a memory, pulsing over the reiterated tone of the fifth, as if this tone of action may carry the composer to other dreams of romance.

Romance

ROBERT SCHUMANN Op. 28, № 2

PART THREE

FURTHER THOUGHTS

This section outlines various approaches used in Creative Motion teaching, to illustrate further how it can be applied to non-music as well as music activities. Brief individual descriptions serve to show the dimension of depth which is added to purely mental comprehension when adequate physical balance freely matches imaginative inner perception.

Adult Class Introductory Remarks

Opal Gilpatrick

The following remarks were made by Mrs. Gilpatrick to an adult class in Worthington, Ohio:

Our bodies are the concrete evidence of our personalities, registering the sum total of all our feelings, our unconscious and conscious responses, and our habits of extraversion.

We register through body *texture:* thick, thin, soft, pliable, wiry; through body *stance:* packed down or pulled up, swung forward or tipped backward; through body *movement:* unrelated movement, which is uneven and forced or related movement, which is smooth and flowing; through our *breathing:* sometimes short, tense, animated, at other times full, rhythmical and inclusive, if we are using a more nearly whole body.

An inspired or fully realized short expression, as in a tennis or golf stroke, or in a good dive, for example, transcends our everyday body habits and allows the body to be one with the expression. All parts of the body will follow through and will be molded into the form demanded by the expression.

By defining the concrete body moving through time and space, the elements of the movement can be analyzed into a statement of the principles underlying the expression. It is these moments of transcendence that every artist and sportsman works toward. Such perfectly timed experiences and inspired moments being usually unpredictable and uncontrollable, we need to build our training process on the underlying principles governing all action.

There are two sides to all experience, the inner thought-feeling strand and the outer body performance. The most fulfilled realizations or the most inspired expressions, are those in which the body is in complete rapport with the demands of the inner thought-feeling projection.

In music, a talented person could be defined as one whose muscles perform what he hears and feels, often despite habits that have been trained into his muscles. Let us examine what is involved. To express in any form depends upon moving the weight of the body in consonance with the body's structure. The most perfect and efficient expression is one in which all the parts work together in relationship with the whole. That is called a timed expression. Everyone has had moments of such complete realization.

My understanding of this process has come from experiencing, and teaching others to experience, music by working from the inner hearing-feeling through body rapport with this feeling and with the instrument being played. My understanding has also grown through the application of the same principles to my everyday living activities. The results, in music, are a more realized performance, a more intimate knowledge and understanding of the art of music than the average student usually achieves, since it evolves from one's own hearing-feeling and not from copying another's playing. The body constantly grows more tuned and more sensitive to the music and to all other forms of expression.

All realized expression is based upon respiration; intake and release. To create form, you use your body with phrasing. A music phrase is a unit replica of respiration, with its impulse (start) and its climax (release). For a phrase to sing, it must be realized through a body respiration (energy respiration not just breath). The impulse is like being in the trough of a wave; you "rest" on the motion of the wave and are carried up by the energy of the rebound to the crest (climax) where you must let yourself go "over the top" and down to the next trough (impulse again). The motion keeps on going, impulse to climax, climax to the next impulse. Phrase thus organizes experience.

Energy mobilizes whole in response to your idea or desire, unless it is interfered with. Start with the radiant whole of the composition singing inside through the first phrase, to get the feeling before you begin to play. Then lift your hands and settle into the first tone. Yawn, and let go what is holding your hands. Then play, relating each phrase to the next. You play the music, not the piano.

The yawn uses energy whole. It is the prototype of our use of energy. It puts potential power all in one place; starting at the center, it takes the inner charge for which we have geared and transfers it into action. Energy takes the yawn to the periphery, the hands, where there must be a yawn also. The body fills in or adjusts to the extension, to keep the diaphragm related. We think of this yawning experience at the impulse as "making the gesture with the diaphragm".

At the climax of the phrase, there must be another yawn, a feeling of "once further" as the phrase is breathed off (released). This constant flow of phrase with the "once further" for each turnover of force actually maintains our Light Weight Body ease. At the center it is like a whirlpool vortex and waves. Like a feeling of intake against a creative power. It is transferred as power, not as yourself. The motion, by exercising the vibratory rates of the body, frees the music to sing. The joy is in hearing those things that you have first sensed.

Snowball Exercise for Preschool Children
Presented at Teacher's Workshop in Louisville by Opal Gilpatrick

The children are seated. Enlist their attention by some statement such as: "I am going to make a snowball for you." Standing before them, I do the exercise as I talk:

"I'm going to roll into a snowball. My head drops down, down, down. My fingers touch the floor. One knee slides behind me. The other knee slides down. I sit back on my heels. I place one hand here (at the sternum). I place the other hand on top, like this. I put the top of my head here on the floor, like this. Now I am a ball!"

"Mary, come touch me gently and roll me over." (I roll out, flat on my back and lie quiet for a moment. The children are delighted. Everyone desires a turn. Turns are allowed, as long as the group interest sustains).

"Now, it is your turn to make a ball for me to roll over." (I give the same directions and follow along with the children, at first. At the end I move about, rolling over each little ball. From the feeling of the body I can tell the degree of "centeredness." The body should be in *equilibrium* around the diaphragm center. The pattern of the rollout indicates the relationship of center to circumference. I don't change that. I watch it grow free as the weeks go on.)

To play the "going up part" of the game, after the roll-out, I say: "Take a big yawning breath against your back and roll over onto your side. Your knees and your head try to touch. Feel your nice stretchy back. Close your eyes. You can feel your back breathe. Now, let another big yawning breath roll you over onto your knees. There, you are a ball again! Then one foot comes forward with the knee at right angles; and with another big spring against the floor you come up to a standing position. Continue coming up until your head balances easily on top of your neck."

How Parents Can Help In The Child's Learning Process

Florice Tanner

Feeling the need for cooperation at home, especially in the case of young children, Miss Tanner addresses herself to parents in specific suggestions.

1. Help your child develop a habit of *releasing energy up and outward before* he starts doing what you have asked him to do.

If he habitually tackles a task with inhibitive, driving, heavy downward energy, he needs help, for that habit will defeat his expression. It will increase insecurities, produce hurry, worry, excessive tenseness eventually even perhaps undermining his health.

Your child can be *taught* to *surmount* worry, fear and their physical manifestation, *excessive tension*. You can help. Do you know how he tackles a new or difficult task? Does he start by holding his breath, clenching his fist or other muscles? Does he, as it were, draw the energy *down* into himself and hold it there, tensely; or does he have the happy habit of letting his thought and energy flow out over the entire task, thus letting his muscles and body be free to follow the line of energy his thought made.

The first impulse on a task is so important, for in it is either the free release of his energy and body, or a clenching, holding, selfinhibiting quality. No task, physical, mental or emotional, can be well expressed with this clenching-down heaviness. All adequate expression is preceded by an outgoing release of energy, which is observable in the impulse to action. Watch the child, especially watch his first impulse in doing something. If this energy release is completely free his body and muscles will follow on the line of energy made by his thought and there will be no excessive tension or insecurity.

2. Help your child be *aware* of the *inner swing* or *motion* of energy in all movement or expression. This awareness to the inner feeling comes *before* action or mental analysis. Parents could help a great deal by playing many games which develop kinesthetic imagination with their pre-school or primary grade children. Example: "Close your eyes and think *how it would feel* to walk like an elephant. Now open your eyes and do it. I'll guess whether you are a big or a little elephant!" Other games could be played imitating anything that moves: a cat leaps, a hen scratches, a robin pecks, a plane banks, a train starts, etc.

Help your child be sensitive to this *inner* experiencing and know, because the inner experience is a pre-requisite to all outer visible expression. If the inner experience is clear, the outer expression is likely to come through a coordinated body and thus be efficient and beautiful. Even more significant, if the inner sensitivity is clearly felt *before* visible action begins, there is greater quietness and security of behavior. Help your child develop this habit of feeling inner security before he starts overt expression.

To train sensitivity have him roll a ball, or swing a pencil, hand or foot, keeping the exact rhythm that flows through the words or music as you recite or sing to your child. Inner sensitivity to the rhythm is essential if the body is to move with matching tempo.

The importance of right timing in our mechanical age is well understood. Timing in the body depends upon the use of proper gearing, the correct body balances for every expression. These balances are set when the energy is released in the initial visible action. When the inner feeling is clear and the energy is released so as to cover the action, the body balances swing on the timing or motion and smooth expression results.

3. Train your child *how* to *listen*. As you give directions, have him *imagine* the feel of doing the job. For creative listening, the body must be alert with energy flowing in a way to make him feel tall, but rested (a vertical two-way-stretch). It is exceedingly important that a child be able to focus his attention at will, so that he can become one-pointed in his attention. You could give him invaluable training at home in your everyday requests if you check these two habits *before* he starts to move. In the beginning he needs help, lest he start to act before the inner experience is clear. Soon he will establish correct habits.

4. Help your child to know *how* to *focus* attention on any part of his body which is tense and then to release energy through that area to relieve the tenseness. It is a conscious letting-go that brings freedom.

5. Teach your child that *inner experience* well mastered shortens the need for visible and audible drill. A child needs the ability to visualize quickly and experience kinesthetically, through imaginative inner work. For example, five minutes away from the piano spent hearing the tones inside and feeling the muscles of the body and fingers which will be used to play the piece is worth much more than the same length of time playing the difficult section over and over. Likewise, in spelling, time spent thinking of the feel of the sounds in the words on a list we have found to yield quicker results than

merely writing or spelling the words. To learn to type, think of the feeling in the whole body necessary to write a certain word; see, in the mind's eye, the whole word and feel the swing of the letters which form it. Repeat this several times; then go to the typewriter and see how much your drill time has been shortened.

6. Teach your child to try consciously to rise above anger, fear, panic and discouragement by deliberately releasing energy over the entire affair before him. This tends to make a balance within the organism which is constructive, secure and outgoing.

When addressing herself to the teacher's problems, Miss Tanner does not directly approach methods of teaching subject matter, but rather seeks to have the teacher understand how to help her pupils self-control and self direction. She does this by training underlying habits of energy release, whereby his energy is channelled into specific tasks. She holds that the great obstacle to learning is faulty energy projection.

Applying Creative Motion In the Classroom (Excerpt)

Florice Tanner and Julia Ostergaard

The following useful applications of the principles have been found to be effective in classroom teaching.
1. Children can attain a basic primary control as their habitual way of functioning or use of body force i.e. a *light weight body*.
2. They can learn techniques which they can consciously use to function with *wholeness* in any given situation or activity.
3. This approach to classroom experience produces greater ease and a higher degree of concentration on significant experiences for the individual and helps mesh the gears of desirable group unity.
4. This approach to learning through the functioning of the whole organism does not preclude or ignore the methods and techniques which all good teachers employ to teach subject matter or to establish favorable room climate. *It does, however, imply conscious responsibility on the part of the children.* In the light of our cultural commitment to the democratic way of life this would certainly be desirable.
5. Teachers can learn these techniques and present this training within the framework of their own way of working with children. It is important to recognize that an adequate understanding of this way of working with children is not likely to be obtained if it is presented *only* on the mental level. Children accept this fact wholeheartedly, but adults must make the effort to overcome deeply entrenched habits, and themselves be willing to participate as both researcher and laboratory.
6. Since much of this training aims to give results at the conscious level which the infant has instinctively, the earlier it takes place, the better.

Reading Aloud

Julia Ostergaard

Reading aloud, in small groups, is an almost universal practice in primary classrooms. All too often, however, children can be seen drooping around a table, in a listless posture, bodies making no contribution to the effort. Or, what is worse, their bodies may be tight and tense, which is no more conducive to effective learning.

Children can be trained to "sit up", but comfortably; to hold a "light book" and to use their bodies to help their reading efforts. The vocabulary for this matters little, so long as it conveys the alert but free-from-excessive-tension posture. The effect on smoothness of line, voice quality and eye movement is, to an alert teacher, readily observable.

To help convince the children, a teacher who knows them can walk a short distance away, turn her back and tell accurately whether or not a child is reading with good posture, according to the criteria which have been set up, and at least partly established. Needless to say, the children enjoy making a game of it and the habits established stand them in good stead.

How Creative Motion Imposes New Responsibilities (Excerpts)

Florice Tanner and Julia Ostergaard

New responsibilities confront the teacher in our changing world. As challenges open new dimensions, new insights need to be developed. The speed, endurance and flexibility demanded by modern times requires of our bodies a finer and finer synchronization of the motion of the parts with the motion of the whole. To train individuals to achieve optimal functioning, new educational techniques are needed.

Research was pioneered by Martha Russell, and teachers in many parts of the country have continued to explore two areas:
1. To find the psycho-physical set which gives optimal readiness for all expression.
2. To recognize the method of the organism's response to a governing idea.

Experience under varied conditions appears to support the conclusions: Children can become aware of different ways of functioning; they are able to feel the difference within themselves and to observe it in others; they can, often with relatively short periods of training, learn techniques which they consciously utilize to help them function with wholeness in any situation or activity.

Balance and stability are needed as a foundation for every type of expression. Early in this work (Creative Motion), it was found that certain psycho-physical responses gave freedom, ease and security. The training which evolved from these discoveries teaches the child to be consciously *aware of how he uses himself.* It also emphasizes that he, and only he, can release energy to be buoyant and free and at the same time physically relaxed. He experiences the feeling and gladly shifts, when he remembers.

Without a detailed description, resilience and balance can usually be obtained by thinking of widening the back as one inhales and allowing the body to elongate as exhalation takes place. The result is readiness for optimal expression and . . . can become a habitual way of life . . . .

Superimposed on this steady state, this habitual way of living, are the many shorter experiences of daily activity. Observation and study in this second area have revealed a similar pattern both in receptive activities, such as listening, and in outgoing activities, such as moving, speaking, organizing, etc. A governing idea, or concept, sets body balances automatically, in relation to the extent, speed, quality, environment and the person involved . . . When the governing idea is clear, these balances adjust throughout the organism, without conscious direction . . . Upon the first step or overt expression, there must be a consciously directed impulse release to *cover* the entire thing to be done. All steps which follow build to a climax, the fulfillment of the concept. At this climax there is another energy release upward and outward and, at the same time, the body rests downward, at ease. To the degree that the releases at the impulse and at the climax lack completeness, the action or expression will lack ease, beauty and wholeness.

The children, of course, do not want anatomical descriptions of what is transpiring. For them it is enough that self-direction gives ease, joy of movement, free expression . . . Vocabulary to describe the interaction of a number of variables does not come easily. Children have been encouraged to make their own phrases to reveal what they are experiencing. Thus, the state of resilience and balance has been called the "light weight" or "light feeling" body, or "getting a feeling of lightness and quietness" or "feeling swingy." They like to remember that they are "trees," not "posts." The teacher checks to be sure they are experiencing a release of energy upward and outward, balanced by the body weight resting downward. "Make a pattern before you start," is the way one group expressed the clarity of the governing idea. "Moving all in one piece," or "streamlined," quite aptly describe a smooth sequence of actions.

At the outset, frequent, short periods of training arouse awareness and interest. Acceptance and enthusiasm follow as children realize that routines become smoother, academic work easier, imaginations more vivid and social contacts more pleasant. To follow directions the first time they are given, to move chairs for a reading group quietly but quickly, to go to the gym or assembly with no need for a discussion of behavior, saves time for pleasant extras. To write more rapidly with less fatigue, to hear pleasant low-pitched voices, to be more comfortable because a yawn and a stretch are accepted, even encouraged, and perhaps (even) to work with a teacher whose enthusiasm is not worn thin, leads to the conviction that "living at one's best" is the good life.

By way of conclusion, there follow excerpts based on Mrs. Russell's notes for talks to her classes. They are as applicable today as when they were written.

Body Tuning

Now we come to the actual training itself; the thing that we are going to do. It makes no difference how you want to use this process of Creative Motion; whether it is for an art form, like music, the dance, or for sports, golf, tennis, swimming; whether it is for business contacts or study, or for outer or inner organization, always the beginning step is physical training. For the body is the medium or transfer station through which creative imagination realizes itself in outer form.

If we suppose then, that the body is tuned to respond to creative imagination, tuned to the same laws of Motion that create the form, then the body must be equipped with a twofold interacting mechanism. There must be something that is the body equivalent for the creative impulse and there must be something that actually puts out, handles and shapes the form. It is easy to see that it is the outside body that does the shaping, handles the form and makes the contact with the world. That much we have to use, whether we will or no, to accomplish anything.

Now what is it in the body that is the body equivalent of the creative imagination? We will find that it is an illusive thing known as tonicity; body tone; an inner readiness. This has been overlooked in nearly all our training. We have sought results without being motivated by an inner vitality spark.

Music should help us in this process. Unfortunately we tend to treat music as mere performance, instead of realizing that music is in reality something we live by, move with, think to. We relegate music to an adjunctive position in education, whereas the concept of music as something intimately bound up with our being and becoming should place it among educational fundamentals. We can develop a technique for music expression through our *experience* of the flow of the melodic respiration of music, since the music's balances are found to be in exact vibratory relation to our own body balances. We have only to grow in increasing perception of these matching balances in relation to the increasing clarity of musical expression, to see how each whole has in its execution the same law of form, the same principle of growth, namely *respiration,* impulse and climax, the creative unit and the constructive unit-working continuously together.

The tuning which music can give our bodies, if we match its flow, is needed for our occupations of every day, to give them beauty and ease. We all experience the marvel when unsuspectingly we tap in on the rhythm of creative energy and things come right. But we need to learn how to do this consciously, not leaving it to inspiration or chance. The only way that we can meet the accelerating tempo of our modern living is by finding that quiet place in Motion, the creative place where the thing is done *before* you do it and then the *doing* itself is without effort and with joy.

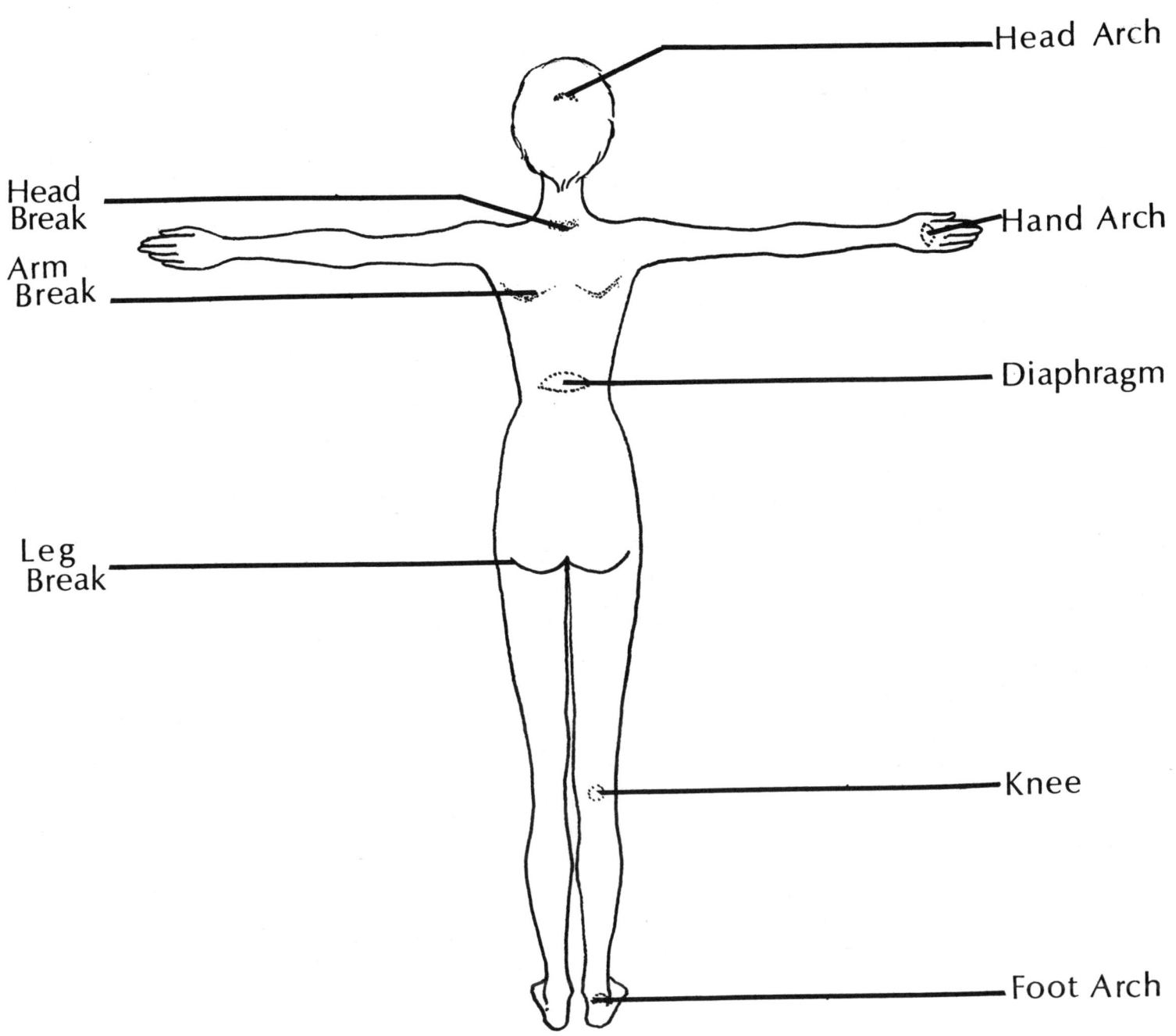

SUPPLEMENT

Martha S. Russell's
General Exercises
Used in Creative Motion Work.

1. Wall Exercise — to strengthen and align back and improve posture.
    A. Stand with back to wall and heels the length of one foot from wall.
    B. With fore fingers on hip bones, thumbs toward back, move thumbs to center of back until you locate the two hollows in pelvic girdle.
    C. Put these points against the wall.
    D. Leaning forward from the waist, breathe open lower back against the wall.
    E. Shift upward against the wall until lower back and diaphragm level are both firmly touching the wall.
    F. If possible, without withdrawing lower back, get shoulders and head also against wall. (Watch that neck is extended, chin in.)
    G. Now bring one foot back to the wall, maintaining the position achieved and walk away carrying the body balanced over arches of feet.
2. Snowball — to encourage correct breathing habits, and tune center to circumference.
    A. Standing, exhale and bend over slowly (knees may bend), head and arms leading until finger-tips touch floor (vertical Line).
    B. Extend one foot back gradually and come to rest on one knee, then lower the other as well.
    C. Now sit back on your heels, with toes in and heels turned out.
    D. Fold hands one palm over the other at the sternum bone (diaphragm).
    E. As you exhale, make a forward gesture with diaphragm bending forward until you are doubled up, elbows relax at sides.
    F. Breathe in and out (lateral and vertical) until body becomes light and starts to sway naturally.
    G. Allow yourself to roll out with a big exhalation; and rest on back.
    H. Still lying on floor, draw up knees, with feet firmly on floor and breathe whole torso, pelvis to top of head, against floor.
    I. Extend one leg, allowing foot to slide along the floor and giving a lift at the leg break to keep from pulling lower back off the floor. Extend other leg in same fashion.
3. Roll — Learning to use diaphragm impulse.
    Lie on one side on the floor, with arms extended above head. Exhale and roll over and over across the floor on diaphragm impulse. Do not push with hands and feet, but keep going with vertical extension on exhalation and lateral extension on inhalation.
4. Getting up on all fours on diaphragm impulse.
    A. Lying flat on floor take a breath and as you exhale roll over on to the side with head and knees drawn close together.
    B. Exhale and as a big breath comes in against your back swing over onto your hands and knees.

(See position finished in your mind's eye, before you start.)
5. Doggie exercise — to establish head and diaphragm connection
    A. Get on all fours, with hands spread out and fingers turned in toward each other about two inches apart.
    B. Exhale, releasing the force from the back of the diaphragm to the front and sweep chin down toward the floor between your hands. (Keep *lower back straight* throughout)
    C. Draw your chin in towards your body, letting head swing way under and releasing the force from the front of the diaphragm to the back.
    D. Continue this release and inhale as the body rises to the full extent of the arms.
    E. To change direction and go down again, take the inside "yawn" that causes the "once further" feeling of lateral extension and release the force in the back of the diaphragm, which allows the chin to move up. Continue releasing, exhale and sweep down again, leading with your chin.
    F. Repeat from beginning several times.
6. Cross-line body set-up
    A. Draw imaginary lines connecting the four points of the feet (from under the big toe to the outside of heel, and under the little toe to the inside of the heel).
    B. Exhale and as your breath comes in, tell yourself to take the best possible position over the center of this cross. Let your body adjust for comfort.
    C. Bring each of the following points over the four points as in steps A and B.
    Foot and leg:
    (1) Arch of foot over cross-over of four points of feet.
    (2) Ankle over cross-over of four points of feet.
    (3) Knee over the ankle over four points of feet.
    (4) Leg break (section through thigh just below buttocks crease) over the four points of feet.
    (5) Pelvis over the leg break, etc.
    Body:
    (6) Diaphragm over the pelvis over four points of feet.
    (7) Arm break (shoulder blade) over **diaphram**, etc.
    (8) Head break (necklace area) over diaphram, etc.
    Head:
    (9) Medulla Center (where spine enters skull) over head break, etc.
    (10) Sphenoid Plane (head center diaphragm) over head break, etc.
    (11) Top of Head over head break, etc.
    (12) Once Further above head over head break (as if suspended).
7. Harmonic beat swings over four quadrants of diaphragm
    A. Exhale and as your breath comes in raise arms above head balancing over center of body.
    B. Soften front at sternum bone as you release force from front quadrant to back quadrant.
    C. Make a yawn and allow arms to stretch high enough to free them above the diaphragm level.
    D. Now release force from back quadrant (under shoulder blades) into front quadrant.
    E. Draw a circle with finger tips in the air releasing first front, then right side then back then left side as you go around.

   F. Draw a figure eight spiral with finger tips starting forward, around to right, back around to center, cross forward to left and back around to center (releasing *each* quadrant as you go).

   G. Repeat the figure eight movement in two whole note harmonic beats. With arms above head
      (1) Yawn, soften at sternum bone, resting all of yourself on the drive of a whole note, swing forward and around in loop to one side. (Fingers take flight immediately and body follows in timing.)
      (2) Another yawn at climax and sweep around the other loop of the spiral.

8. Leg Exercises
   A. Leg throw connecting diaphragm with arch of foot.
      (1) Lie on back with knees raised and feet on floor.
      (2) Exhale and with arch spring against the floor, raise right foot allowing knee to bend upon chest without pulling. (Toes are cupped up and instep leads foot.)
      (3) Now yawn and throw bottom of foot towards the ceiling and out forward, being careful not to allow small of back to come off the floor, extend leg as far as possible and down to within a foot of the floor.
      (4) Yawn again to reverse the energy to instep (top of foot) and return with foot cupped, knee flexed but not pulling (leg break must be open and free).
      (5) Repeat several times on each side.
   B. Cross-Over Leg Throw — To strengthen use of leg break.
      (1) Lie on floor with left leg stretched out and right knee flexed, foot on floor.
      (2) With spring against floor and yawn throw right leg over left with toes pointed toward the floor (keep both sides of pelvis in contact with floor throughout) the stretch comes at the leg break.
      (3) Yawn again to reverse the force and return foot to floor.
      (4) Repeat several times alternating legs.
   C. Baby Exercises.
      (1) Lie on floor on your back. Roll knees up towards your head until you are balancing at your diaphragm level. Fold arms over legs at knees. Now spring legs up into air.
      (2) Lie on back. Roll knees up onto abdomen. Spring legs into air with your pelvic stabilizer (buttocks), keeping pelvis on floor.
      (3) Lie flat on back, with knees flexed and feet on floor. With your pelvic stabilizer spring up that portion of your body between leg break and diaphragm, but keep diaphragm itself on the floor.

9. Combined Arm and Leg Exercise
   A. Lie on floor with right knee flexed and right hand resting on right knee.
   B. Exhale and as breath comes in yawn and throw arch of hand and arch of foot up towards ceiling, then sweep them apart to full extension but do not go down to the floor (lower back must remain flat on floor).
   C. Now yawn to reverse the force in hand and foot, cup fingers and toes, allowing knee and elbow to bend without pulling, return hand to knee (keep elbows close to side of head).
   D. Repeat exercise with the other arm and leg.
   E. Repeat exercise crossing left hand to right knee and vice-versa.

10. Arm and Hand Exercises (Keep arm break open all day. Start with fullest extent possible.)
    A. Arm Break Respiration to Music
        (1) With arms extended forward and palms of hands together, give "once-further" squeeze of arches, yawn on count of 1-2-3-4 feeling lateral extension, in hands and arm break.
        (2) Release on climax of phrase with another yawn 5-6-7-8 feeling vertical extension through entire body, especially in hands and arm break.
    B. Weight-lift Pantomime (Shows connection between hand and arm break.)
        (1) Holding an imaginary string with a weight tied on the end between your fingers and thumb in front of you, yawn and with a lateral extension of hand and arm break, lift weight slowly about two feet.
        (2) Release with another yawn and lower the "weight" with a vertical extension.
    C. Arm and Hand Spirals (To clarify lateral and vertical feeling in relation to use of arms and hands.)
        (1) Lateral Spirals
            (a) With right arm extended in front, palm down, yawn, releasing force from arch of hand to outside edge of finger-tips and with a lateral feeling in arm break, sweep through a loop to right, down, out, up over, turning hand over in its flight. Now yawn again to reverse the force and sweep through the left loop, down, out, up over, turning hand up as you come to the crossing.
            (b) With left arm in reverse manner
            (c) Using both arms in opposite directions, leading with outside edge of finger tips, swing loops to left and right, then cross arms to swing other loops.
            (d) After the full arm swings do fore arm swings and wrist swings and finally finger swings.
        (2) Vertical Spirals
            (a) With right arm extended palm to left, yawn releasing force from arch of hand to outside edge of finger tips sweeping up to the left over upper loop, then with another yawn and hand turned out drop down to the left and around the lower loop.
            (b) With left arm extended palm to right, yawn releasing force from arch to outside edge of finger tips and with lateral extension sweep to right up and over upper loop turning hand palm up as top of loop is reached, then with another yawn to change the force, swing down through lower loop.
            (c) Now do the same exercise with (1) *fore arm*, (2) *wrist* and (3) *fingers*. You may hold elbow with other hand for #1 and #2. You may hold hand at wrist for #3.
    D. Elbow Weight-Balance Exercise (for head and shoulder set-up).
        (1) With arms bent and fists doubled up close to shoulders and weight in elbows, yawn to release force into elbows, raising them forward, up, out and back.
        (2) Yawn again, reversing force to sweep elbows down and back as close to the body as possible, exhaling completely. (Be sure that you have a Light Weight Body and that the lower back does not cave in.)
    E. Hand Respiration (Good for piano technique to limber up fingers.)
        (1) Sit at table. Place hands palms down in front of you, fingers extended.

(2) Think "once further" into table, yawn to release force from the inside arch to outside and allow arch to rise to fullest extent letting fingers slide together, but never leaving surface of table.

(3) Yawn again, reversing force to inner arch and slowly lower center of hand to table. The fingers gradually slide out until they lie flat once more.

(4) Repeat several times.

F. Hand Turning Exercise. (This gets you "on top of" your hands.)
   (1) Stand with arms extended, palms together.
   (2) With a yawn throw little fingers up, pivoting on thumbs and bring hands together back to back.
   (3) Now bend elbows and swing hands (still back to back) down and point them at your chest.
   (4) Starting at the wrists begin to separate hands as you extend forearms forward until only the tips of the fingers are in contact. (Inhale as you execute this maneuver.)
   (5) Now exhale with a yawn and bring arches of the two hands firmly together.

G. Flat-Finger Exercise — Gives independent finger control and strength.
   (1) Seated at table lay one hand palm down with fingers extended.
   (2) Rest down "once-further" into table with center of first phalange (first the thumb, then each finger in turn) and allow finger to spring up from the point at which you "rested".
   (3) In the same way "think once further" up and allow finger to return smartly to table.
   (4) Repeat the same with the second phalange and the finger tip — all fingers and thumbs.

H. Finger Extension.
   With both hands held before you, palms turned in, do scissors with fingers starting with little finger and ring finger, etc.

I. With elbows bent and fingers held up do "bicycle" exercise with each finger in turn.

J. Finger Contact
   Clip fingers and thumb together smartly. Do it up and down in different note values and rhythmic patterns.

K. Finger Bending — *Keeping other fingers extended* hold if need be.
   (1) Bend fingers one at a time as far as possible, close to base.
   (2) Bend fingers one at a time across to base of thumb.

L. Hand Throw on Arch Spring. Piano interval stretch preparation.
   (Both hands simultaneously).
   (1) Resting thumbs on table, with fist closed, take a yawn in arches of hands and let fingers extend on the throw, using thumbs as pivots.
   (2) Yawn once again and release force from finger tips. They will curl back into fist.

11. Foot Exercises
   A. Flexion and Extension
      (1) Stand with weight balanced over four points of feet.
      (2) With lateral extension raise arches to highest extent.
      (3) With vertical release lower arches allowing furthest possible extension of feet.
   B. Ankle Rotation. Standing, with four points of feet firmly fixed rotate ankles out, then in,

without moving the knees.
- C. Knee Rotation.
  - (1) Standing, with arches over four points of feet, rotate the knees outward, with lateral respiration.
  - (2) Relax, and then rotate them again.
- D. Leg Break Rotation.
  Standing again with body firmly balanced over four points of feet, take lateral and vertical respiration focusing on leg break.
- E. Toe Exercises (feel arches over toes). (Help with fingers if needed.)
  - (1) Extend toes to the side, one by one. Then return.
  - (2) Lift toes up one by one, lowering them with a "ping".
- F. Walking Exercise to note values.
  - (1) Step on left foot.
  - (2) As right foot comes down, roll up left foot (crinkle heel), focus on little toe side as foot rises.
  - (3) Move left foot (swinging from free leg break over arch).
  - (4) Lower left foot to floor, focus on inside pad of big toe coming down.
- G. Treading.
  - (1) Stand with feet together, toes straight forward, right foot flexed.
  - (2) With a yawn send the force from left arch to the right arch, causing left heel to spring up and right heel to go down with weight.
  - (3) Repeat this sequence several times, being careful not to pump with the knees, it is a transfer of energy from one arch to the other. (Keep pelvis level throughout.)
- H. Boot Exercise — To limber up heel and ankle.
  - (1) Sitting on chair with legs crossed, grasp right foot with left hand and right ankle with right hand, as though about to remove a boot.
  - (2) Wiggle foot with rotary motion as though trying to remove a boot.
  - (3) Reverse process with the left foot.

Flat-Finger Work

Written by
Martha S. Russell

August 14, 1944
New York City

As always happens after a period of intensive teaching, new vistas have opened in the Motion work, and I want to hand them on to you at once, incomplete as they necessarily are at present and incapable as I am of adequately describing them at any time. They reveal the amazing relationship that exists between energy gearing and body breathing, and the place the latter takes in the TOTAL RESPIRATION economy; in fact, may complete the Motion picture itself, making clear the simple way in which we are supposed to make good our inner energy gearing in our outer action living. I shall set down what I found in the order in which I worked it out.

I began with the regular flat finger exercise, keeping palms flat on table, raising fingers alternately counting four. Then I added the release "pressure" on one and two. It was at this point that, observing inner reactions very closely, I noted a strange thing. Every now and then the downward pressure and the upward finger stroke would happen simultaneously, in a flashing instant, which was not what I meant it to do of course, but when it did, a seeming miracle happened. The release down-pressure stroke was no longer a muscular action but an indescribable inner "charge," as if, as once upon a time some of the physiologists held, there was actually brain-stuff in our body as well as in our head, and that little inner charge was the finger *thinking*. In response to that thinking — no, let's cut out the word response for there was no separation in time, the two things happening in the same instant — flash, the finger lifted — apparently without volition on my part, and certainly with no effort — and a calm and an all-pervading peace settled through my mind and body. That all-pervading calm is the hallmark of the real thing, and so comforting that the practice of "body thinking" is taken out of the realm of "exercises" to become a practical pursuit.

It took me two days to get the down stroke thinking for the upstroke finger, and the upstroke thinking for the downstroke finger localized and operative. My head-thinking of what I wanted done would again and again miss its connection with the finger-thinking that put through the job; besides, it was highly concentrated work; I had literally to "feel" my way, and in the beginning it seemed as if one's inner attention span could never be brought to the place where it would function easily and continuously, for any length of time one might desire. But after a short space one's inner attention steadies and one begins to find it operating without conscious direction; in this new evolutionary departure, we have again compassed the cycle: "from unconsciousness, through self-consciousness, to consciousness," and just as we begin to despair of the ability of the inner attention to stand the strain, the connection between head and body thinking that has been in arrears begins to assert itself and the body thinking is free to settle back once more into an instinctive, but now self-realized response.

The other thing that was puzzling in the flat-finger work, was the localization of the thinking charge. I couldn't find out at what point it happened. So, I went over the four levels of that finger work again and again, and now I can tell you where to put your focus of attention from the beginning and save yourself a lot of time. The flat finger exercise itself, is the basic one which frees the entire finger action from the metacarpal hinge to the finger tip and your focus of body-thinking should be at the focal point of the finger contact — in this case about the center of the second phalange. At this contact point your *finger thinks down,* i.e., "once further" in the direction it was going, at the same instant that the finger lifts. At this same point on the back of your finger, your finger thinks *up* at the same instant that your finger drops. It will probably give you trouble in the beginning to hop your finger thinking rapidly and definitely from the front to the back of the finger, so count to four, or six and take it slowly. The three contact levels on the third phalange that give the increasingly lifted hand are handled the same way. I found it was very comfortable to do these exercises as I lay in bed at night, on my back, with my arm stretched out lengthwise beside my body; the relaxation, the darkness seemed to raise my "feeling" perception several degrees, while the whole experience was restful and a grateful preparation for sleep. When the single fingers begin to work more easily, begin on intervals, i.e., two fingers at once; 2nds, 3rds, etc. And when you begin to get freedom in this, connect them; then go back again to the single finger work and beginning with the first and second fingers, play them in melodic connection. I found that it was better to keep one's finger-thinking to the finger that was *down* at the moment; it seems to be easier in the beginning to think "once further" against a concrete surface than against the air. Carry this on into the various intervals, i.e., 2nds, 3rds, etc. successions and you'll have something in the way of technique that you never knew before. This finger-thinking technique carries into the fundamental key-contact and key release exercises of course, doing away with any chance of *physical push* or pressure on the key, and the correspondent body drop.

Light Weight Body Maintenance

After my discovery of the "finger thinking" release, my mind was off on other explorations — to the prototype of hand respiration, i.e., body breathing. I applied the same technique to lung respiration. It was difficult to do at first because there was nothing concrete, like a table or keyboard contact to help one out, and to become aware, entirely through inner feeling, of the point in the inhalation and the exhalation of one's lung breath at which that "once further" thinking occurred, took some doing. I finally got it through the feeling of the Figure Eight spiral in the breathing. Now it is so simple and so definite that I can't think why I made such a fuss about it. You do a steady and continuous lung respiration to a count of two or four — the count is just to give stability and evenness to the flow of breath. At the instant the inhalation releases, (and vice versa) *think* the inhalation (or exhalation, as the case may be) "once further!" You will presently find that you have established a deep-lying, fundamental breathing that relaxes, tones your physical body, unsnarls your nerve's tensions, and clears the direct energy of your mind. You see we have maintained that energy respiration and body respiration were two different things, and have given an exercise for making clear that though they operate together at the impulse and climax of action, in between these the lung breath goes on its own way, but we have never shown — or known what the lung breath did while it was on its own, nor why it did it. It now appears that this fundamental lung respiration is the breathing, or action correspondence of the Light Weight Body. That it is actually this fundamental of our lung breathing that is designed "with every breath we draw" to re-create and sustain our light weight body stance! You can see why, in the beginning, I said that the discovery of the uses of body breathing in its creative motion relationship, completed the cycle of my findings on the Motion of Respiration. For, as you will see for yourself presently, lung or body respiration is the action counterpart of energy respiration; just as energy respiration has its fundamental light weight body gearing, so the body respiration has its fundamental light weight body breathing; and just as energy respiration in response to the "governing idea" lifts the fundamental body gearing to the required energy gearing of the moment, so the body respiration in response to energy gearing, lifts its fundamental rhythm to the melodic respiration pattern I spoke of in the beginning.

THIENSVILLE EXPERIMENTAL SCHOOL, Thiensville, Wisconsin, 1932

Excerpts from Report

General Summary

...The body class, besides its roll of freeing the body (body tuning), presents an analogy for building up a unified, objective attack on all of the children's problems: academic, psychological and social... He becomes a whole person, organized for "intake and out-put."

Arithmetic Application

....Rolling a ball to certain numbers, until a child is able to make the ball roll on the curve of the number he wishes and can *feel* in his body the *quality* of the number.

....Knowledge of unit quantities: 1+1+1=3 objects on through beat measure and bar lines in music.

....Concrete number understanding through musical games.

....Reading and writing of numbers. After the body is tuned to the number by rolling a ball, the number would be written on the board.

....Working in this way, the number work is closely related to other subjects, instead of being a separate, differentiated study.

....Learning that each one of us goes on his own rhythm and on his own curve.

CREATIVE MOTION STUDY IN HORACE MANN SCHOOL, 1939

Excerpts from Report to Donors

We are happy to be able to tell you that Creative Motion has made a startling record.... It is important to the ongoing work in education to have what we now have, a body of data illustrative of this power, in terms familiar to the present day educator. We have the results of standardized tests, pictures of the children, samples of their work, phonograph records of their voices and teacher's evaluations. In all of these, the Motion children show much greater gains.

Physical Gains

....We begin by showing the posture pictures of the children, because they are so dramatic. Those who have seen the pictures, have expressed interest and amazement, both at the prevalence of such extreme faults of body set-up in an otherwise favored group, and at the changes shown by the children in the Motion group, at the end of six months.

....Fourth, and most important, all of these children have lost that peculiar look of lack of *wholeness* in their bodies.... Instead they show an awareness of being pulled together, of head and body being one and interoperative.

.... In no case has the new awareness of body meant an increase of self-consciousness, but rather the opposite. The children are now taking their bodies from place to place, instead of being taken by them.

Academic Gains

.... The Motion group shows an average gain of more than twice as many points in I.Q. as the control group (10.5 as compared with 5.0)

.... an average Mental Age growth on the part of the Motion group of 1.5 more than the control group. In the fall the average I.Q. of the control group was higher than that of the Motion group, while the opposite is true in May. This points clearly to the importance of Creative Motion as a factor in releasing even so subtle and little understood a thing as "mental aptitude."

Behavior Gains

.... These indicate that the Motion children were definitely ahead of the control children ....

BALTIMORE GROUP

(A report to a student of Mrs. Russell)

June 24, 1947

Dear Mrs. Buckler:

Enclosed please find two copies of the results of the testing of the "Buckler Group".

As you read the results, you will note certain striking changes in the children. I was particularly interested in the personality aspects and was impressed by the fact that, in general, all the changes indicated were in the direction of more acceptable behavior and more wholesome attitudes both toward self and toward social situations.

But now a very serious word of caution: we are not justified in ascribing these changes to the course per se, for these children have been living in many ways during the five months — at home, in school, etc., and their experiences have been gained from all of these sources. In other words, experiences in addition to those received in the class, have been wide and varied. We can probably say however, (1) that the changes in personality were all in the same direction and this might not have occurred in a group selected at random, and (2) that these changes occurred in an environment and at a time in their lives when this type of instruction was a part of their plan of living. What I am trying to do is to caution you against direct cause and effect relationships, yet I do want to suggest that we must think of the inclusion of this element in the environment which produced similar changes in several children. If the ones who were absent at the second testing can be corralled, I shall be glad to test them also, providing they finished all or most of Mrs. Russell's course.

Very truly yours,
L. Kathryn Dice, Psychologist

Mrs. H. Warren Buckler, Jr.
1002 Bellemore Road
Baltimore 10, Md.

About The Authors

MARGARET B. ALLEN

Margaret Belknap Allen, in her early years, moved into the world of music in a natural creative way. Previous to any professional training, at the age of five, she was improvising on the piano, intuitively expressing four part harmony, and rounding out the tonal meanderings with a certain amount of phrase form. Fortunately her first teacher, the then noted Mrs. Crosby Adams of Chicago, was a pioneer in the imaginative and creative approach to music training. This, of course, nurtured the child's inherent urge, so that soon after her lessons began she startled her father (sitting next to her in church) by singing the harmonic structure of the hymns rather than the words. "Quiet now" he would whisper. Later, at the age of ten, she organized a club in Oak Park, where she lived, teaching her interested peers to improvise.

Oberlin College and the University of Wisconsin left their strengthening stamp upon her: but she was always haunted by the wonderment of "why music moved as it did?" "what was the inner necessity that made the rules of music effective?" The casual answers never seemed to satisfy her.

While she was teaching Interpretive Dance and Drama in Evanston, she met Martha Russell and became acquainted with the Creative Motion principle with its necessity of involving the whole self in order to experience the needs of the music. At last dance, drama, rhythm, melody and harmony all moved together in a wholeness of expression.

After marrying John Milton Allen they moved to Scarsdale, New York. Here she taught in her private studio for sixteen years, inspiring the students to hear inside that which the music actually wanted them to hear on the outside. The response and the results justified the approach. Following the death of her husband, and after her daughter and son had left home for their further education, she chose to transplant herself to a college campus where the student's background was different from those of Westchester. Berea College invited her to teach in the Music Department where she has taught for twenty five years, interrupted only in order to get her Master's degree at Stanford University. She eventually became professor of Humanities and Piano, but it was always the Creative Motion principle that guided her teaching.

As a little Scarsdale boy once said to her: "I hope you never die" she realizes that those who truly experience Creative Motion gain something "which makes all of the difference" not only to their music, but to their selfhood.

Margaret B. Allen

ANNE W. NILES

Born in Baltimore, Maryland, living in a professional family atmosphere as a doctor's daughter, Anne Williams Niles showed no disposition to carve out a career, but nevertheless entered into her conventional schooling with enthusiasm, under the excellent leadership of Miss Edith Hamilton at the Bryn Mawr School.

Beginning with the nursery songs she learnt from her mother, she was always interested in music, and early began taking piano lessons. There was little encouragement, however, until her final year of school, when she came under the inspiring influence of Martha Russell, who opened for her a whole new dimension of understanding.

She continued her studies at Wellesley College, until her marriage to Emory H. Niles, a young lawyer who later served Baltimore as Chief Judge. They have a son, two daughters and eight grandchildren.

Even before leaving school there was volunteer work at a settlement house run by the Alumnae Association. This was followed by working at the Johns Hopkins Hospital, serving on Boards such as Planned Parenthood, League of Women Voters, Fund Raising and teaching in Church School. Always there has been concern for social justice and peace. In every field she encountered the same conflicting interests and waste of effort, especially in educational areas.

Fortunately, Mrs. Russell, from whom she had learnt the principles of Creative Motion, returned to Baltimore, so that lessons with her could be resumed. Thus it became possible to learn more about the process of teaching by assisting in the class work.

Later she began teaching on her own, working at first with small children's groups and later with adults. Also, at annual Windswept Workshops under Opal Gilpatrick and Margaret Allen she deepened her understanding by being both participant and teacher.

Her experience has convinced her that Creative Motion offers practical and effective ways of dealing not just with music, but with the varied activities and problems of life. By harmonizing mental impulses and body responses it "teaches us the path from inner working of governing idea to outer expression."

Anne W. Niles